Functional Education
for Disadvantaged Youth

Committee for Economic Development

Supplementary Paper Number 32

OTHER TITLES

in

the CED Series

on URBAN EDUCATION

Edited by Sterling M. McMurrin

RESOURCES FOR URBAN SCHOOLS:
Better Use and Balance

Supplementary Paper Number 33

(April 1971)

THE CONDITIONS FOR EDUCATIONAL EQUALITY

Supplementary Paper Number 34

(May 1971)

FUNCTIONAL EDUCATION for DISADVANTAGED YOUTH

Edited by
Sterling M. McMurrin

Ralph W. Tyler
Garth L. Mangum
Seymour L. Wolfbein
Howard A. Matthews

Heath Lexington Books
D.C. Heath and Company
Lexington, Massachusetts

A CED SUPPLEMENTARY PAPER

This Supplementary Paper is issued by the Research and Policy Committee of the Committee for Economic Development in conformity with the CED Bylaws (Art. V, Sec. 6), which authorize the publication of a manuscript as a Supplementary Paper if:

a) It is recommended for publication by the Project Director of a subcommittee because in his opinion, it "constitutes an important contribution to the understanding of a problem on which research has been initiated by the Research and Policy Committee" and,

b) It is approved for publication by a majority of an Editorial Board on the ground that it presents "an analysis which is a significant contribution to the understanding of the problem in question."

This Supplementary Paper relates to the following Statements on National Policy issued by the CED Research and Policy Committee: *Raising Low Incomes Through Improved Education (1965); Innovation in Education: New Directions for the American School (1969)*, and *Education for the Urban Disadvantaged: From Preschool to Employment (1971)*.

The members of the Editorial Board authorizing publication of this Supplementary Paper are:

This paper has also been read by the Research Advisory Board, the members of which under the CED Bylaws may submit memoranda of comment, reservation, or dissent.

While publication of this Supplementary Paper is authorized by CED's Bylaws, except as noted above its contents have not been approved, disapproved, or acted upon by the Committee for Economic Development, the Board of Trustees, the Research and Policy Committee, the Research Advisory Board, the Research Staff, or any member of any board or committee, or any officer of the Committee for Economic Development.

CED RESEARCH ADVISORY BOARD—1970

Foreword

Among our educational tasks, none is more crucial or more difficult than providing the disadvantaged youth of our cities with education that will prepare them for productive employment and guarantee them the satisfactions of a full life. They must have both opportunity and encouragement to pursue college and university programs which will qualify them for the professions and for positions of leadership in commerce, industry, and government. At the same time, education must open the doors to positions in every walk of life and at every level of the economic structure to ensure that no one is denied employment and the opportunity for advancement because of deficiencies of the schools. This goal is a long way off. To reach it will require action now.

Fortunately the traditional ideas of vocational education are yielding to the realities of economic life—the necessity for technical and semi-technical preparation for most jobs; the rapid obsolescence and changing character of job functions and the necessity for basic training that facilitates change and mobility in the worker; the increasing automation of production that reduces the demand for blue collar workers and increases the need for education for services. Education for the jobs of the future must provide basic knowledge and cultivate the capacity to learn. To increase human understanding or the capabilities of effective communication is often more important as preparation for successful employment than the development of specific skills.

This means that there is not a great distance between today's "technical" education and education of the more "academic" variety. Both should be designed to prepare the student for a productive life in the world of work; both should provide him the ground for cultivating his intellectual capabilities to a high level; both should nourish his originality and creativeness, refine his sensitivities, and help him to invest his life with meaning and purpose. The choice between "technical" and "academic" schooling should not be a choice between poor and good education. Rather, it should be a choice among the various patterns of life, the diversity of occupations, which education opens to the individual. The task of the schools is to make those options real and viable. The disadvantaged no less than the advantaged must have educational opportunities that will lead to employment at all levels of technical and professional ability. Considering the disheartening conditions that now exist among the disadvantaged, the deplorable lack of economic opportunity, and the persistent failure of society to provide that opportunity, that task is gigantic. But it is one in which success is demanded.

The present volume is concerned primarily not with the options available through higher education, but with effectively tying schooling with jobs to ensure employment. Certainly a necessary condition for success is the coming together of education, industry, and business in joint ventures that combine basic academic instruction with the practical experience and on-the-job training which will not only qualify the student for employment but will, in fact, guarantee that employment. Too often the vocational and technical schools of the past have prepared people for work which did not exist, or trained them in skills already obsolescent, or brought them to the threshold of employment which they were denied through discrimination.

The success of a joint venture of education, industry, and business on a scale large enough to make a real difference will require extensive public funding and adventurous experimentation with new ideas and new ways of doing things. It is now clear that more money spent in the same old way will not solve our educational problems. More money is indeed needed, but it must be invested in new ways of educating. Numerous experiments are proving successful and near successful on a modest scale, but, as Garth Mangum's paper clearly shows, the present fragmented and scattered experiments must be brought into some coherent order and given strong organized support.

It is the special merit of the papers which compose this volume that they dig deeply into the problems of "functional education," to use Ralph Tyler's felicitous term, in search of new and better ways. Their authors write from different backgrounds of experience but each with expert knowledge, and they bring diverse perspectives to the central issue: how to bring disadvantaged urban youth into the mainstream of our technologically and industrially grounded society and break the cycle of poverty in which they are caught.

These papers were commissioned by the Committee for Economic Development as part of a more general study of urban education, which resulted in the policy statement on *Education for the Urban Disadvantaged: From Preschool to Employment,* issued in March 1971. They are published here separately from the other research papers of that study because the subject with which they are concerned deserves special consideration and attention.

Sterling M. McMurrin, *Project Director*
Dean, Graduate School
University of Utah

Contents

Functional Education
for Disadvantaged Youth

1. The Concept
of Functional Education

Ralph W. Tyler

Under appropriate conditions, the vast majority of youth can learn the skills, habits, knowledge, and attitudes required for employment in our modern industrial society. Yet for many young people, the essential conditions for learning the things needed for occupational competence are not to be found.

Learning of a positive sort requires the effort and involvement of the learner. Prodded by external force, he can learn to *avoid* certain behavior—not to cross the street, not to take things that attract him, not to express his views to those who punish him for the expression. But force is an ineffective incentive to learn to *do* something, especially to acquire complex skills such as reading, writing, diagnosing breakdowns in a machine. For a person to put forth the effort to learn and to be actively involved in it, he must perceive the learning task as significant and worth doing, as well as something that he is capable of doing. As he attempts to learn, he must recognize that he is making progress and that he is becoming successful in doing what he has undertaken; he should obtain satisfaction from this success. Most importantly, if what he is learning is to become part of his normal repertoire of behavior, he must find opportunities in his daily round of living to use what he is learning and to have continuing practice in it.

3

It is this that is often lacking today—the informal and unplanned experiences that once provided youths with constructive participation in occupations. Formal education must now fill this gap. Occupational education should begin in the primary grades and evolve over the years. Education must be recognized by the students as helping them to deal with life, and the curriculum must be designed to serve this purpose. The school must not remain isolated from the rest of the community if it is to play its part in vocational-technical education. At present, a majority of our youth are not properly prepared for participation in the world of work, but ways to improve this situation are available and have been tried in scattered places. What is needed now is a comprehensive reform.

Occupational Education Yesterday and Today

In earlier generations, young people living on farms or in small towns observed the processes of production, distribution, and consumption firsthand. In most homes, children easily recognized that work was required of all able-bodied members of the family in order to eat, sleep, and have a clean household. Most of them also learned early and at first hand the habits and attitudes required to get the chores done properly and on time, and they saw their parents involved in various kinds of necessary work. They were also familiar with many aspects of the division of labor characteristic of the time—farming, housekeeping, retailing, road building, lumber making, teaching, nursing, preaching, doctoring—and they recognized some of the differences in these occupations. Furthermore, they shared in the consumption of the products of these vocations.

These experiences gave children of the past a simple picture of an economy. They could see the role performed by agriculture, retailing, and some of the service occupations. They recognized that these were necessary roles. They could also observe some of the kinds of activities carried on by the practitioners. As children, they talked about these jobs and which ones they would want to have when they grew up. Not only did they explore some vocations in fantasy, but as they grew into adolescence they had opportunities for part-time jobs during the school year and full-time work during the summer. This furnished tryouts of several kinds of work carried on in their community and established a further basis for understanding the world of work, for appreciating the contributions made by different occupations, and for recognizing the requirements for employment in various jobs.

During the process of growing up, every normal child and youth develops a picture of the world and relates himself to it. The experiences he has in the home and the community provide a basis for this world picture, although the impressions he receives from television, from the movies, and from reading help greatly in expanding and in filling in details of his map. When his experiences are limited and when the mass media are inadequate or inaccurate in depicting important sections of this world map, significant processes, institutions, and relationships are lacking or greatly distorted. Thus, when I was a boy growing up in a small Nebraska town, my schoolmates and I had a fairly clear and accurate picture of those parts of the economy that were strongly represented in our community—farming, retailing, and the community service occupations. We also realized that some things we used—such as soap, sugar, wagons, stoves, and washing machines—were made in factories in other states and were shipped in by train. Thus, we recognized that factory workers and railroad employees had significant work to do. But we had only vague and mostly sinister notions about "the bankers," "Wall Street," and "the giant corporations." They were viewed as wolves extorting money, goods, and services from those who were really productive. Most of us looked forward to obtaining employment in an occupation that we thought was a necessary one, in jobs that we thought we could handle successfully and would be happy and proud to carry on. Thus, we gained a constructive occupational orientation at an early age in relation to those significant occupations we saw in our world picture.

As we grew up, our experiences in and out of school helped to shape our vocational choice. If we found school work dull and uninteresting and if we were being given failing grades in school, we dropped out as early as we could in order to get a full-time job in which we could gain satisfaction from our work and income. If we found school tasks enjoyable and rewarding, and if our parents emphasized the greater rewards of jobs requiring high school or college graduation, we remained in school and made plans for occupations that were open to those with more education.

In past generations, the school did not provide specific job skills or knowledge. These were acquired on the job either by trial and error or by apprenticeship. This was true of professional and managing jobs as well as skilled, semiskilled or unskilled ones. One of the chief contributions of the school to employment was to serve as a sorting institution. Children and youth were expected to do educational tasks at the same rate, regardless of differences in background, modes and rates of learning, and styles of attack. Those who met the teachers' expectations most fully were given high marks; those who met them least well or not at all were given failing grades. Those with low marks got farther and farther behind until their discouragement led to their dropping out of school and finding employment.

When I was in high school, only 10 per cent of the age group remained for graduation and only 3 per cent went on to college. The composition of the labor force at the turn of the century was such that most jobs were unskilled and could be filled by dropouts from the elementary school. Only a small portion of the jobs required a college education. Hence, schools and colleges that sorted out students, and did not attempt to educate those who had not already developed interest and competence in learning, were appropriate for the society of that time.

As science and technology have been applied at an increasing rate, the economy has become more complex, society has become more urbanized, and the composition of the labor force has greatly shifted. Most young people now have little basis for building a world picture that properly represents the various occupations, their roles, the jobs they involve, and the characteristic activities and requirements of these jobs. Interviews with children indicate that less than half know what kinds of things their employed parents do. They perceive their parents or the government as "giving" them food and other necessities. Few have any conception of the division of labor or of an interdependent economy. Most jobs are seen as a source of money but not as an essential contribution to the society. Corporations, banks, owners of oil wells, and stockbrokers are thought to be unnecessary or even pirates in our society.

Lacking an orientation to the modern economy, many youth do not think that acquiring the skills, the knowledge, and the attitudes required to be employed in an occupation is worthwhile, although these may be necessary in order to get money to live. Not only do many young people fail to see the significance of an occupation, but they also have little or no comprehension of what one must learn to pursue it. If they enroll in programs of vocational or technical education, they do not have clear learning objectives and they lack confidence in their ability to acquire the skills, knowledge, and attitudes involved. Their efforts to learn are frequently aimless and they gain little satisfaction from their progress. Nor are they motivated to continue practicing what they are learning until this becomes part of their normal repertoire. In brief, many students do not acquire vocational or technical competence because the necessary conditions for learning have not been provided. What is required is a thorough reexamination of the total process by

which one can prepare effectively today for constructive participation in an occupation.

Occupational Education Evolves from Childhood

From their earliest years, children are building a picture of
the world in which they live; an important part of a real picture is that of the economy. Since many modern processes and
institutions of production, distribution, and consumption are
not readily observable, special attention must be given to experiences in and out of school that will enable children to perceive
and understand the ways by which they obtain necessary goods
and services. Lawrence Senesh has shown in the experiments in
Elkhart, Indiana, that first grade children can easily grasp such
concepts as the division of labor, medium of exchange, production and consumption, distribution, and transportation. Children in the primary grades likewise can gain a simple working
understanding of the roles of capital, credit, or insurance.

To develop a constructive orientation to the world of work,
it is not enough to tell about it, read about it, or even present
pictures about it. Initial experiences need to be ones in which
children directly participate—work involving the varied efforts
of several children and adults. The meaning of an economy is
clearer when a child wants a product or a service, and by helping
to produce, distribute and consume it, finds that he can surmount some of the difficulties in these steps by such processes
as division of labor, getting credit, or borrowing supplies and
equipment. As the child gains some of these direct experiences,
his understanding can be broadened by sharing with others
through discussion, or by exploring more complex examples of
these processes through reading and viewing films. By the end
of the fourth grade, most children should have developed a
"picture" of the modern economy that is an accurate depiction
in the main of major economic processes and institutions.

This kind of orientation cannot be successful if children are confined wholly within the walls of the school. Children in the primary grades should be observing and participating in economic activities in the community, where significant experiences can be had and where they can meet and work with other youths and with adults. Thus they can share in the economic life of the community at the same time that they try out simple occupational activities.

This sampling of occupational experiences for children should be designed particularly to include technical and service occupations, in which employment opportunities are increasing for the very reason that these are less commonly understood by youth. In the past two decades, the proportion of the U.S. labor force engaged in the production and distribution of material goods has sharply diminished while the proportion engaged in service occupations—education, health services, recreation, social services, accounting, administrative science, and engineering—has greatly increased. The occupations for which the demand is growing are those requiring social and intellectual skills. Those for which the demand is dropping require physical strength and manual dexterity.

The largest number of children in our schools come from a working-class background. Although girls from this group perceive themselves as developing social and intellectual skills, the boys see themselves as developing physical strength and manual dexterity. Hence, the girls generally anticipate going into service occupations; the boys do not, viewing such jobs as "women's work." As a result, 60 per cent of the new jobs that became available between 1950 and 1960 were filled by women. It is very important for boys to sample service jobs, so that they may discover that they can do this kind of work successfully and that it can be rewarding. In this way, the child's picture of the world of work will include not only the processes, the institutions that perform them and their values, but also the kinds of work individuals do in the various parts of the economy, the activities carried on, what it takes to perform these activities, and what personal pains and pleasures arise from this work.

The first five years of schooling should also enable each child to develop habits of work that are basic to all group endeavors whether in work, at home, or in socio-civic activities. These include getting to the job on time; beginning activities promptly and carrying them on energetically during the assigned periods; operating in ways that minimize interruptions or damage to the activities of others; and checking one's efforts periodically to see that adequate results are being achieved. Many children develop these useful habits through the opportunities and discipline provided in the home, but many do not. Through a broadening of its program, the school is in a position to instill these habits in those who do not have opportunities elsewhere and to afford a wide range of situations for practice by all.

By the fourth or fifth grade, the school should encourage and help children to test more systematically their dreams or ideas about what they will be when they grow up. Choosing a career is neither a discrete event nor an irrevocable one. Not only do children and youth continue occupational exploration and planning over the years, but many adults rethink and replan their occupational future. Under favorable conditions this is a good thing. As the economy changes, and as we gain more adequate understanding of the world of work and of ourselves, newer and better opportunities may be identified and our goals and plans adjusted accordingly.

However, certain steps are well-nigh irreversible under present conditions. In some of the large city school systems, the curriculum which the child takes in the middle school or the junior high school will make it impossible for him to gain the high school education required to go to college, to take technical or subprofessional post-high school programs, or to enroll in vocational-technical curricula in the high school. In school systems where the "streams" are not so rigidly formed, the judgments made by the children, their parents, their teachers, and their counselors on the basis of their elementary school performance often direct them into educational programs that commonly prevent the children from getting the educational opportunities that would enable them to take jobs they could learn to handle and for which there is demand.

The correction of this serious defect in our schools requires not only reform in our guidance and track systems but also the development of an educational program that helps children and their parents to understand the range of opportunities available and how to carry on continuing occupational selection and the educational planning related to it. Many people are very vague about the educational or training requirements for the main kinds of jobs. They do not know which entry jobs are likely to be dead-end, which can lead on to a career progression. They do not understand the ways in which education can be planned to provide an initial base on which further education can be built on various time schedules such as full-time study through high school, college, and professional school; part-time study while employed on an entry job; alternation of terms of full-time employment and full-time study (cooperative education), and other schedules distributing periods of education and employment in different ways over several decades of life. The five-year period from ten years to fifteen years of age is an excellent time for the school to encourage the student to develop occupational and educational plans.

He can be aided in his learning by making systematic studies of several classes of jobs which interest him so that he can find out whether they are open-ended or dead-end; what training is required for entrance; what later training, if any, is helpful in promotion; where these training opportunities can be had; and what prerequisites there are to obtaining the training. If there are persons in the community who hold such jobs, students should talk with them and, where possible, sample units of instruction that illustrate such training programs. Several hours each month could be used fruitfully in helping students carry on systematic exploration of occupations and jobs that seem attractive to them so that career choices will not be superficial, educational and training needs will be anticipated, and students can learn how to continue life planning over the years.

In the high school, the emphasis should be on developing job skills that will enable the student to fulfill the requirements of one or more classes of entry jobs, to broaden and deepen his understanding of the current "world of work" and its problems, to enhance his appreciation of the contributions made by the major types of occupations and the pleasures and pains of various kinds of jobs, and to continue his occupational and educational planning. Although many vocational-technical fields require post-high school education, the current adolescent "hang-up" is partly a reaction to the years of schooling unbroken by experience in a full-time job. For many adolescents, the high school and post-high school years of education need rescheduling so that young men and women may leave school, work, then return to school, later go back to full-time work in various work-education patterns. If attention is not focussed on assisting students to develop marketable skills in high school, their frustrations continue when they drop out of school and fail to get meaningful jobs.

Beyond the high school, vocational-technical education needs major review and reconstruction. It suffers from too great a separation between theory and practice; between education in the classroom and the understanding, skills, and attitudes developed through experience on the job; and between the instructors' teachings and what students learn from each other. From the standpoint of effective learning, post-high school education suffers from the lack of clear educational objectives, inadequate conditions for learning, and the assumption of uniform group progress in learning. An important step in improving the situation would be a wider adoption of cooperative education—an educational arrangement in which the student has alternate terms of full-time employment and terms on the campus, with both employment and course work designed to complement and supplement each other. This generally leads to a redesign of the curriculum, a clarification of objectives, greater individualization of instruction, and a wider use of other aids to learning, both human and physical. Most students preparing for technical and service occupations will be involved in post-high school programs.

All Effective Education is Functional

This paper is devoted to vocational-technical education. Hence, it focuses on those aspects of schooling required for effective occupational education. It is not the author's intent, however, to suggest that there is any difference between the conditions required for students to learn things which will enable them to carry on successfully their occupational activities and the conditions required for learning things helpful in other areas of life. The conditions essential to one kind of education are essential for all kinds. Unfortunately, they are not met in the case of a substantial number of students.

In spite of the need for educated people, the high school fails to serve effectively more than half the youths who are of high school age. Over a million of them drop out each year before completing high school, and an equal number of those who remain make no measurable progress on standard tests in high school subjects. Of those who stay on until high school graduation, one-third do not develop the skills, habits, and attitudes required for higher-level employment and for civic leadership. Our failure to educate such a substantial number of students is not due primarily to their inadequacies but rather to the inappropriateness of the program to supply them with the kind of learning they need. They are concerned with becoming independent adults, getting jobs, marrying, gaining status with their peers, and helping to solve the ills of the world. They can see little or no connection between the educational content of the school and their own concerns. "What has geometry to do with life?" they ask. "Why should I try to remember the chief battles of the Revolutionary War?" Even the high school science laboratory appears to them to be a place for following the directions of the laboratory manual to see if they can obtain the results reported in the textbook.

Because they do not see the relevance of the high school curriculum to their present and future lives, they do not become actively involved in the learning tasks assigned. They turn their attention to other things such as athletics, social activities, and artificial stimulants, or they become quiescent, enduring the school routine until they can drop out.

One factor standing in the way of developing educational programs that students can readily see as functioning in their own lives is the tradition that the high school should be an adolescent island outside the major currents of adult life. Modern society has increasingly isolated adolescents from the adult world. Yet this is the time of life when young people are looking forward to being independent adults; they need opportunities to work with adults, to learn adult skills and practices, and to feel that they are becoming mature and independent. Hence, the restrictions on youth employment, the limited opportunities to learn occupational skills at home, the segregation of civic and social activities by age groupings—all these add to the difficulty of the adolescent and increase his anxiety about obtaining adult status and competence. The high school should help to bridge this gap.

To do so involves the development of a close, active relation (not simply a formal one) between the school and the responsible adult community so that the student can apply what he learns in school to the questions and problems outside the school. The emphasis of functional education is upon learning those things that are relevant to his life, not upon earning grades, credits, and other artificial symbols. This does not seek to make the school identical in content, activities, and organization with life outside the school; the school can be used as an institution to help the students learn the things that are needed in dealing with life outside. As an institution that can guide and facilitate learning, the school becomes a resource for obtaining knowledge, ideas, questions, procedures, skills, and attitudes that help students meet the opportunities and problems of life. The school is by no means the only place where the student learns; but it ought to help him learn effectively and efficiently those things that have been discovered, formulated, or refined by scholars that are useful in his efforts to deal with life successfully.

To make school education functional, we must furnish high school students with opportunities to carry on significant adult activities—job programs, community service corps experience, work in health centers, apprentice experience in public agencies, research and development agencies, and in other situations where significant problems are being faced and important work is being done, and where learning is an asset. It is necessary to redesign the high school in order to open it to the community and to utilize many kinds of persons to contribute to this educational effort. The school will need to serve a wider range of ages and to allow students to vary the amount of time devoted to studies. To supply a substitute for grades and credits as qualification for employment opportunities, a certification system will need to be developed to validate the student's competence in various major areas. This will also tend to reduce the emphasis upon purely formal requirements such as class attendance and the completion of prescribed courses.

Functional education is not a simple formula and therefore may be misunderstood. It involves using work and other arenas of life as a laboratory in which young people find real problems and difficulties that require learning, and in which they can use and sharpen what they are learning. There is no intention of substituting learning on the job for the deeper insights and the knowledge and skills that scholars have developed. The teacher, the books, other materials of the school, and the intellectual resources of the community are to be employed by the student as he works on the problems of his job and carries through projects on which he is engaged. When he is actually doing work that he finds significant, he can see for himself, with the aid of those who know the field, that many kinds of learning are helpful and even necessary. Coordinators are needed to connect education with the world of work, and teachers must learn to select the content of school subjects and assist students to use it in connection with the activities in which they are engaged.

The student is concerned with civic and social service activities as well as with gainful employment. In these areas he will meet problems that involve values, ethics, aesthetics, public policy—in fact, the many facets of real life. The opportunity is thus provided for the student to comprehend the perennial areas of educational concern, which encompass social and civic understanding and commitment, health, personal integrity, and the arts, as well as the skills of occupational competence.

To provide for the varied interests, abilities, and career plans of students, corresponding variations can be made in the selection of school assignments related to the job and in the division of the student's time. For example, John Brown, a well-read student, who has been very successful in most of his previous school work and plans to enter a university, might work twenty hours a week for one year in an industrial laboratory and another year in a community service corps providing supplementary educational services to the children of an inner city area. He might be taking advanced high school courses, or he might be doing independent study in one or two jobs. On the other hand, Tom Smith, a student who is skeptical of book learning and the relevance of schooling to his life, might work twenty hours a week in a data processing center for one year and another year in a community health center. His school studies should furnish a basis for finding other interests to be pursued in more intensive study, perhaps helping him to select a technical institute for further occupational preparation.

The proposal assumes an extension of the hours per day and weeks per year devoted to high school education. The present five- or six-hour day, even in concentrated vocational laboratories, is little enough to satisfy the level of skill now required for job entry. With the proposed variety of activities in and out of school, the student should be able to work eleven months per year without undue weariness. Since he would receive pay appropriate to the service rendered, summer vacation jobs would not be important.

Some of the major features of this proposal are currently used in imaginative programs of vocational-technical education in some high schools. Unfortunately, even in these cases the benefits are limited to the few students enrolled in these programs. But they demonstrate the feasibility of work programs, wider adult involvement in the education of youth, and closer relation between learning in school and activities outside. Parts of the program have been employed in various places and subjected to impartial evaluation.

The kind of education described here has been shown to arouse greater interest and effort in many students than classroom study alone, to increase student understanding of the subjects studied, and to develop maturity of responsibility and judgment. Community service corps experience such as that developed by the Friends Service Committee has been found to arouse in many students greater motivation to learn and to develop social skills, social responsibility, and maturity of judgment. Some communities have constructed a neighborhood Youth Corps Program to serve a similar purpose with young people from backgrounds of poverty and limited opportunity. The involvement of a broad range of people in the educational activities of youth has proved helpful as has the provision of a variety of patterns to include, in addition to full-time enrollment, part-time school attendance while holding full-time or part-time jobs, and enrollment in high school, full- or part-time after a period of work, military service, or other activity. This varied pattern of experience and competence can be utilized constructively in an institution open to the community, whereas it is likely to be a handicap to a school operating in isolation, with study confined to textbooks and related materials.

The development of such a program involves the construction of a new school curriculum, the making of new institutional arrangements, and the training of persons for new positions and new roles.

Changes Required in the Curriculum

Functional education requires a different curriculum emphasis from the present one but it does not merely substitute out-of-school experiences for academic training. It recognizes that children and youths, when given an opportunity to do so, learn things that are meaningful to them and appeal to them as significant. When subjects seem to them irrelevant, alien to their experiences and interests, or unimportant, students give them little attention and do not put forth the effort to learn. Furthermore, when they learn things that they cannot continue to practice, this learning soon disappears and does not become part of their normal pattern of behavior. Hence, the curriculum problem is to help the student to recognize those subjects that are significant and to arrange experiences that will enable the student not only to learn these things in school situations but also to practice what they have learned in various relevant situations outside the school.

Obviously, children learn many important things outside the school, but the school has particular responsibility to draw upon the knowledge and wisdom developed by scholars, present and past, in identifying things important to learn that are not likely to come to children's attention in their activities outside the school. The school has the further duty of helping children to use these resources of scholarship in living more constructively, more intelligently, and with greater personal satisfaction than is possible without them. The basic skills on which the elementary school focuses its attention are good illustrations of important contributions of scholarship that can enrich their lives—reading, writing, mathematics, study skills. History, geography, economics, and science also can furnish important sectors of the "world picture" which children are creating. These and other content subjects can provide concepts that are helpful in understanding situations which youth meet today and are useful in solving problems which they face.

Each subject deals with certain kinds of questions and problems, and particular ways have been devised for seeking to answer these questions and to solve the problems with which they deal. Hence, the content of school subjects need not be perceived as dead and inert, but rather as active fields of investigation that can furnish helpful tools for people to use today. The objectives of functional education are to help the students learn what the several subjects have to offer that can be significant for them, how to use these resources, and how to develop habits of using them. These objectives are important for all education including vocational-technical programs.

Since the contents of most courses of study and most textbooks have not been selected with these objectives clearly in mind, schools run into difficulty when they adhere too closely to most prescribed courses. Hence, a major step is required, namely, a review of the potential content in each major subject and the identification of such elements as concepts, questions, problems, and skills that can contribute functionally to the ways in which children and youths live, carry on their activities, and deal with their problems. This becomes the potential content of a curriculum for functional education.

Following the selection of objectives and the identification of relevant bodies of content, the school curriculum can be organized in different ways. Broadly, there are two approaches:

organizing the school program around the different subjects—
e.g., a course in reading, one in mathematics, or one in biology
—or organizing it around projects, tasks, enterprises, or jobs.

In the primary grades, the study of the world of work could
be carried on largely as a major part of the social studies courses
that are commonly included in the present curriculum. The program developed by Lawrence Senesh demonstrates the vitality
and appropriateness of this focus for the first three grades. In
addition, children's interest in learning about the production
and distribution of things they consume stimulates their practice of reading when simple but accurate reading materials
dealing with these subjects are used. The children's oral and
written reports and discussion of experiences involving occupations and the contributions of work are sound bases for practice of oral and written language. Arithmetic is also relevant.
Take as an example a simple project in which children first work
individually to produce the product and then try producing it
through division of labor, with each child responsible for a
specified part. As the children try to find out the amount of
time saved or the increase in production that the division of
labor made possible, counting, calculating, and projections are
naturally in order. This is only one of many possible illustrations
of the relevance that studies of this sort can give to mathematics.

In the middle grades, where the emphasis is upon occupational and educational planning, school time for the program
could be taken from the guidance periods, or the equivalent of
one day a week of the time now allotted to the social studies
curriculum might be devoted to the program. Occupational and
educational planning are easily recognized by students as real
and vital. This content therefore could serve to interest children
in the middle grades not only in reading materials describing
and explaining jobs and preparation for them, but also in stor-
ies, poems and plays that vividly illuminate the contributions
of various jobs, their conditions and their pains and joys. In the
middle grades, students also will find mathematics helpful in

planning the cost and the returns from alternative ways of preparing for jobs that appeal to them. This immersion in various occupational fields may inspire students to explore further what activities are carried on, what education is required, and what results might be expected if one became a scientist, an engineer, a nurse, a writer, or an editor. Teaching is particularly relevant. Children and youth at all grade levels not only can explore the occupation of teaching by serving as tutors for other children but also can make a real contribution to the learning of children. The work of the National Commission on Resources for Youth in its Youth Tutoring Youth projects has demonstrated that those who do the tutoring learn substantially more than those who are tutored. Having accepted a tutoring job, the tutors became very active learners of the subjects they were to deal with in their *tutoring*. These subjects had become functional for them.

In the high school where a wider range of work experience must be made available, greater changes in the curriculum will have to be made in order to provide for the program proposed. Some teachers have constructed courses which emphasize those elements of their subjects clearly relevant to the experiences and interests of their students; they also help their students find applications in out-of-school situations. The possibilities of such courses may be more obvious in subjects such as biology, the social sciences, and literature, but successful courses also have been developed in the other school subjects. The students are encouraged to discuss their experiences in work, in the home, and in other life situations in terms of the seeming relevance of things being learned in their courses. The teachers follow up these discussions with assignments that help students see other connections and use what they are learning more fully.

Curriculum organizations that are based on the projects and jobs of the students require more daily planning and opportunistic selection of relevant subject content than those that are comprised of courses in the several subjects. As students undertake projects and jobs, the teachers serve as consultants, suggesting things that can aid the students and acting as coaches in helping them learn the things they believe will be of assistance in their work on their projects. This organization appeals to most students because it is more real, their need for knowledge or skills being recognized before they attempt to learn what they need. However, because the teacher's role is quite different from the role customarily played in the traditional organization of subjects, it may be harder for the teacher to adjust to the new setting and to get a feeling for his adequacies and inadequacies.

The teacher's work in the classroom must be supplemented by a program linking the school and the community. The development of effective cooperative work-study education requires surveys of local job opportunities. Coordinators must be trained to work with employers in outlining job experiences and their relation to the educational resources of the school. Their primary concern is the utilization of job experience to enhance the student's development. In many cases, a community service corps will need to be established to provide young people with opportunities for social service.

Many school people and parents fear that a new and unorthodox educational program will not be recognized by colleges or employers. However, the criteria for college admission have broadened greatly from those of the early 1930's, when it was common to prescribe the courses to be taken and require an examination based on specified textbooks. Present policies prescribe broad fields of study and examine a candidate's verbal facility and ability to handle quantitative relations. Furthermore, employers now rarely look for particular courses or kinds of high school programs in considering job applicants. Nevertheless, the program recommended here would be more easily adopted and developed if there were an acceptable means for certifying the educational achievement of the students. Tests and other devices are now available to measure educational accomplishments in terms of most of the knowledge and skills that contribute to success in college or competence in handling a job. Federal government support of the development and standardization of tests of competence in various major areas of learning would help in gaining approval of the necessary changes in the schools and also provide a means to institute the certification system.

The establishment of this program in many states may require modification of child labor laws to permit a student to do work related to his schooling. Similarly, practices and attitudes among employers and labor organizations will need to be changed, but earlier work-study programs and some of those developed for disadvantaged youth demonstrate ways in which they can be effected without too much burden to employers and other employees. Precedents indicate that all of these problems are soluble ones.

2. Preparing Youth for Employment: The Role of the Public Schools

Garth L. Mangum

Bettering the employment prospects of inadequately educated American youth has been a priority objective of federal manpower, antipoverty, and, to a lesser degree, education policy since 1963. Yet programs to implement those policies have never been large items in federal budgetary allocations. In state and local policies, the employment problems and prospects of disadvantaged youth have been minor considerations.

From its initial concern with the plight of the technologically-displaced adult family head in 1962, federal manpower policy shifted to a youth emphasis in 1963. The legislative evidence was the aborted Youth Employment Act, the more successful amendments to the previous year's Manpower Development and Training Act, and the Vocational Education Act of 1963. The Economic Opportunity Act carried the youth emphasis into the antipoverty program in 1964. The following year the Elementary and Secondary Education Act attempted for the first time to concentrate additional federal education resources where the help was most needed—primarily those urban school districts carrying the greatest load of children from low-income families and culturally deprived homes.

As the "social dynamite" of 1962 exploded into the actual riotings and burnings of 1966 and 1967, more and better jobs for youth in the ghetto became a clear priority. The Job Opportunities in the Business Sector (JOBS) program and the Vocational Education Amendments of 1968 were responses. Yet for all the legislation and the policy declarations, there has been remarkably little improvement in objective employment prospects and experiences of young men and women from the central-city slums. Ghetto unemployment rates have declined in a reasonable relationship to those of the total labor force, but these rates remain typically three to four times those of the surrounding suburbs. Despite complaints of a labor shortage, one-third or more of the labor force in a central-city slum will be unemployed, sporadically employed, or employed at wages too low to pull the family out of poverty.

The nature of the ghetto labor market has been clarified as surrounding labor markets have tightened, but the problems, though better known, are little closer to solution. The home environment is often a handicap to education and employment preparation; the quality of the schools is often abysmal. Vocational education in the ghetto is no better (and probably no worse) than all education in those locations; moreover, it is limited to the final years of high school after many have dropped out. Limited amounts of postsecondary vocational-technical education and manpower training are available, but the reward for participation is a hunting license, not a job. Well-paid, semi-skilled, and manually-skilled jobs are multiplying, but not in the central cities. Inadequate transportation, housing discrimination, and economic obstacles too often place these out of reach of the ghetto residents. The growing jobs in the central cities either require a high degree of preparation or are unattractive and poorly paid. At current rates of economic activity, it is a rare central-city area which does not have jobs going to waste. But ghetto youth are neither more nor less rational than anyone else. They ask, "Is the job worth taking?" and given their limited financial commitments and alternative income sources they often answer, "No!" Or if a job seems to offer no future and there are plenty just like it available, they accept the job when convenient and abandon it when inconvenient.

Any solution to the employment problem of ghetto youth must do more than provide work skills and employment services. It must open up realistic and believable avenues into the mainstream of the American economy. Employment problems at the entry to the labor market are not unique to ghetto youth. Youth in depressed rural areas have even more critical problems; but they are less concentrated, and their difficulties are therefore more easily ignored. The unemployment rates for all youth are triple those for the rest of the labor force, but for most youths unemployment is a temporary stage as they experimentally seek out their niche. Since most make out reasonably well, it is instructive to examine the process by which they are prepared for and enter the labor market. In that perspective the needs of ghetto youth may be clarified, a philosophy for ghetto education can be devised, and specific actions for implementing that philosophy can be prescribed.

The Role of the Schools in Occupational Training

To understand the persistent lack of success in bettering the employment experience of ghetto youth relative to those from middle-class society, it is necessary to review how most American youth are prepared for employment and then compare that norm to the ghetto environment. The school system must be given major credit for the relative ease with which most enter the labor market, but specific efforts to prepare youth for employment are a minor consideration. The contribution is more accidental than intentional.

As Rupert N. Evans has put it so well, American education is primarily "school for schooling's sake."[1] As a generalization, each level of the system except the graduate school has as its primary objective the preparation of the student for matriculation at the next higher stage of the education system. With the minor exception of a few vocational high schools and post-secondary technical schools, only the graduate and professional schools are specifically and primarily vocational in their purposes. Elementary and junior high schools have only one objective—getting into high school. Again quoting Evans, there are three standard tracks at the high school level: (1) the college preparatory, which carries the primary emphasis; (2) a limited amount of real vocational education, which by and large does prepare a carefully selected few for employment; and (3) the general education track, which leads nowhere but has as its function the incarceration of those who have no particular objective. That which the system assumes to be the goal of all is actually the destination of a few. Of each 100 entering the ninth grade today, 77 finish high school, 40 enter college, and 20 are graduated.

The concept of a vocational education system is largely a myth. There is a federal Vocational Education Act with an accompanying appropriation and a federal bureau to dispense the funds. There is the American Vocational Association and there are state boards of vocational education. There are reports which certify, for instance, that over 7 million persons studied vocational education in 1967. But any relationship to a system ends before it reaches the schools and the students.

The federal act provides funds that, when matched by the states, can be used by the latter to support vocational courses in the public schools. With nearly $50 billion devoted annually to education in the United States, the total federal, state, and local expenditures for vocational education in 1967 was under $1 billion. Prior to 1963, vocational education was restricted to training in a limited number of occupational categories. Though training for any occupation requiring less than a bachelor's degree is now authorized, movement away from the traditional categories has been slow.

During 1967, 3.5 million of the 7 million enrollments were

in high schools, mostly in the junior and senior years. Any attention given to preparation for employment earlier in the school system was not supported by vocational education funds. One-half million youth were enrolled in vocational agriculture, 1.5 million were in home economics, 1 million were learning office skills, and one-third million were enrolled in trade and industry courses. However, this does not mean that these and the small numbers enrolled in distributive, health, and technical courses were necessarily preparing for employment in these occupations. It means that among the classes in which they were enrolled there were one or more classes which were partly supported by vocational education funds. The home economics girls are pursuing the occupation of housewife, but cooking and sewing skills no longer rank high among the necessary qualifications. A limited number of the Future Farmers of America probably intend to pursue farming as a lifetime occupation. Many of the registrants in typing and shorthand classes will use those skills in the business world, but they are as likely to be acquiring them for classroom use. More of the trade and industry, distributive, health, and technical enrollees are seriously pursuing vocations, though many, like the boys in the auto mechanics courses, may be pursuing avocational interests and escaping classroom regimen.

The term, vocational high school, conjures mental images of shop-filled buildings and total dedication to skill training. Such schools exist, but they serve a minor part of the enrollment and face criticism for providing their students with inadequate citizenship training, cultural enrichment, and academic skills, and for segregating them from the "mainstream." In total about 15 per cent of high school students enroll at some time in vocational courses, but far fewer can be counted as having been prepared by the schools for employment.

This is not intended to fault the dedication and the competence of vocational leaders and instructors. Personal observation would give them high marks for ability and enthusiasm. Neither is it a criticism of the quality of the equipment and the course content. These vary widely, usually being good where all education is good and of poor quality in areas where all education is poor. It is only to say that high school vocational offerings are, with minor exceptions, far from a system of preparation for employment.

This is not true for most of the half million who enrolled in postsecondary vocational courses in 1967. Office skills accounted for two-fifths of the enrollments, trades and industrial skills for one-fourth, technicians for one-fifth, and health occupations for one-tenth. By and large, the enrollees had made a vocational choice and were pursuing it. The 3 million adults registered in part-time courses were also, for the most part, pursuing specific vocational objectives, either the upgrading of present or the acquiring of new skills. For those with the motivation to engage in these skill acquirement activities, prospects are good, but postsecondary enrollees are 4 per cent and the adults are 3 per cent of their respective universes.

This recital may cause one to wonder why more youth do not find themselves with employment handicaps. Yet most make the transition from school to work with little difficulty. Most of the differential between youth and adult unemployment rates can be explained by the frequent entries, exits, and reentries into the labor market. Those who complete college are still a small enough proportion of the total to be in demand. Employers must find employees. The schools do provide the basic competencies which are as relevant to reading work and safety rules or operating instructions as story books. Specific skills can be learned on the job and whatever additional skills the student has accumulated are bonuses. Even the child of a successful, working father has a more difficult time becoming acquainted with the world of work than did a farm youth or a person who lived near an industrial plant. But at least he knows that work is central to his father's life and is expected of him in adulthood. He also has relatives and friends who can provide contacts and access to jobs. Better preparation might increase his chances for success, but he has a great deal going for him already.

Since the ghetto youth lacks many of these informal supports, he is more in need of formal preparation. He is more likely to come from a broken home without the example of a steadily working father, and he is less likely to have successful working neighbors as role models. He is in school fewer years and his school years teach him less. He lives in the central city, while the semiskilled jobs he could fill are growing in the suburbs. Around him are two kinds of jobs, those that require more education than he has and those which are lowly paid, distasteful, and offer little prospect for advancement. It is not surprising that his unemployment rate is double the rate for whites of the same age and four or five times greater than the average for the total labor force.

The manpower programs and other employment assistance introduced in the last few years have played a significant remedial role, but they have made little impact upon the basic problem: the accumulation of obstacles and handicaps which isolate the ghetto youth from the unprecedented opportunities offered the well-prepared in American society. More could and should be done to better the employment preparation of all American youth. It is critical that the ghetto youth (and other youth from disadvantaged backgrounds) be given better preparation to compensate for their handicaps and the absence of some of the informal supports so important in the relative success of others. There is already evidence that disadvantaged youth, lacking other help, profit more from current vocational education than others; but what they have is too little, too late, and wrongly oriented, given their needs. Education and training cannot solve such problems as discrimination, location, and transportation, but they can build the attitudes and provide the skills required by attractive central-city jobs.

A Philosophy for Vocational Education*

Only a generation ago, education for most of the labor force was irrelevant to employment. With the exceptions of a few professions and a few skills, the schools had objectives other than preparation for work. Many of the older half of the current labor force are products of that system. In a complex interaction, rising educational attainment has swollen the supply of talented labor encouraging development of a technology structured to use such labor, thus increasing the competition and decreasing the opportunities for the undereducated. In this environment the traditional educational skills of spoken and written communication, computation, analytical techniques, knowledge of society and man's role in it and skill in human relations are all determinants of employability. At the same time, if education is preparation for life, employability skills are essential to it. Practically every member of the population at some time participates in the labor force. Yet vocational choice, like marital choice, is a crucial decision made casually and with inadequate information.

Experience with innovative programs provides increasing evidence that vocational education has more to offer as teaching method than as training substance. Emerging from its initial role as preparation for professions, education has fostered and rewarded the verbal skills important to those pursuits, in preference to manipulative skills and problem-solving attitudes. Lecture and discussion have been emphasized in preference to learning by doing. Federal law which mandated a separate administrative structure for vocational education and defined it as less than college level did not create the separation between

---

Author's Note: This section (pages 31 to 37) was written by the author several years ago when serving as a member of a national advisory commission on vocational education. While the comments were addressed in general to the entire school system, the author feels that they are not only still timely but also particularly applicable to the problems of education in the ghetto. [2]

academic and vocational education but it has certainly perpetuated it. It is paradoxical that the very phases of education which are the most specifically vocational in nature, higher and graduate education, are held in esteem while occupational preparation at a less than college level is without prestige.

Increasingly, both academic and vocational education lose relevance separately. The fusion of general and vocational education does not automatically create instructional content which is more palatable to the student. It is when the student perceives the information as meaningful in helping him to achieve sought after goals that instructional content becomes attractive. Molding an academic package around a core of practical skills capped with work experience provided by cooperative employers seems to offer the ultimate in relevance, particularly for those from deprived backgrounds with limited verbal skills and short time horizons.

Relevance starts with realistic objectives. Vocational goals of students, to the extent they have any, are a product of parental pressure or of supposed glamour which lead to high rates of attrition and feelings of failure. A considerable emphasis is being given to programs directed at helping students to establish realistic goals. This essential pragmatism is the motivation for earlier introduction and orientation to the world of work, improved counseling and guidance techniques, and exploratory programs. Once again, federal law must accept some blame for irrelevance. Though it is common to accuse vocational educators of resisting change by training for obsolete skills, it should be remembered that it was federal legislation, relevant in its day but unchanged over time, that locked the system into the occupational structure of 1917. Those with a vested interest in that structure could not be expected to strongly advocate change. That impetus had to and must come from without.

Finally, freedom can be operationally measured only in terms of the options available to the individual. Ignorance, poverty, disease, and discrimination are major constraints on that range of choice; and education and training are crucial to their elimination. The responsiveness of the school system to the needs of all labor market entrants and participants—the drop-out, the high school graduate, the postsecondary student, the upgrader, and those in need of remedial help—expands or contracts the options and opportunities for self-realization.

From these philosophical concepts emerge five operational principles:

1. Vocational education cannot be meaningfully limited to the skills necessary for a particular occupation. It is more appropriately defined as all of those aspects of educational experience which help a person to discover his talents, to relate them to the world of work, to choose an occupation, and to refine his talents and use them successfully in employment. In fact, orientation and assistance in vocational choice may often be more valid determinants of employment success, and therefore more profitable uses of educational funds, than specific skill training.

2. In a technology where only relative economic costs, not engineering "know-how," prevent mechanization of routine tasks, the age of "human use of human beings" may be within reach, but those human beings must be equipped to do tasks which machines cannot do. Where complex instructions and sophisticated decisions mark the boundary between the realm of man and the role of the machine, there is no longer room for any dichotomy between intellectual competence and manipulative skills and, hence, between academic and vocational education.

3. In a labor force where most have a high school education, all who do not are at a serious competitive disadvantage. But at the same time, a high school education alone cannot provide an automatic ticket to satisfactory and continuous employment. Education cannot shed its responsibilities to the student (and to society in his behalf) just because he has chosen to reject the system or because it has handed him a diploma. In a world where the distance between the experiences of childhood, adolescence, and adulthood and between school and work continually widen, the school must reach forward to assist the student across the gaps just as labor market institutions must reach back to assist in the transition. It is not enough to dump the school leaver into a labor market pool. The school, along with the rest of society, must provide him a ladder, and perhaps help him to climb it.

4.   Some type of formal occupational preparation must be a part of every educational experience. Though it may be well to delay final occupational choice until all the alternatives are known, no one ought to leave the educational system without a salable skill. In addition, given the rapidity of change and the competition from generally rising educational attainment, up-grading and remedial education opportunities are a continual necessity. Those who need occupational preparation most, both preventive and remedial, will be those least prepared to take advantage of it and most difficult to educate and train. Yet for them, particularly, equal rights do not mean equal opportunity. Far more important is the demonstration of equal results.

5.   The objective of vocational education should be the development of the individual, not the needs of the labor market. One of the functions of an economic system is to structure incentives in such a way that individuals will freely choose to accomplish the tasks which need to be done. Preparation for employment should be flexible and capable of adapting the system to the individual's need rather than the reverse. The system for occupational preparation should supply a salable skill at any terminal point chosen by the individual, yet no doors should be closed to future progress and development.

Upon these principles, in turn, one can base a unified system of education for employment, integrating the strengths of vocational and academic education and on-the-job training:

1.   Occupational preparation should begin in the elementary schools with a realistic picture of the world of work. Its fundamental purposes should be to familiarize the student with

his world and to provide him with the intellectual tools and rational habits of thought to play a satisfying role in it.

2. In junior high school economic orientation and occupational preparation should reach a more sophisticated stage with study by all students of the economic and industrial system by which goods and services are produced and distributed. The objective should be exposure to the full range of occupational choices which will be available at a later point and full knowledge of the relative advantages and the requirements of each.

3. Occupational preparation should become more specific in the high school, though preparation should not be limited to a specific occupation. Given the uncertainties of a changing economy and the limited experiences upon which vocational choices must be made, instruction should not be overly narrow but should be built around significant families of occupations or industries which promise expanding opportunities.

All students outside the college preparatory curriculum should acquire an entry-level job skill, but they should also be prepared for post-high school vocational and technical education. Even those in the college preparatory curriculum might profit from the techniques of "learning by doing." On the other hand, care should be taken that pursuit of a vocationally oriented curriculum in the high school does not block the upward progress of the competent student who later decides to pursue a college degree.

4. Occupational education should be based on a spiral curriculum which treats concepts at higher and higher levels of complexity as the student moves through the program. Vocational preparation should be used to make general education concrete and understandable; general education should point up the vocational implications of all education. Curriculum materials should be prepared for both general and vocational education to emphasize these relationships.

5. Some formal postsecondary occupational preparation for all should be a goal for the near future. Universal high school

education is not yet achieved but is rapidly approaching reality. Postsecondary enrollments are growing, and before many years have passed, the labor force entrant without advanced skills gained through postsecondary education, apprenticeship, or on-the-job training will be at a serious disadvantage. Universal advanced training will bring increased productivity, higher standards of living, and greater adaptability, to the profit of the economy as well as the individual. If postsecondary education and training is to be universal, it must be free. Fourteen years of free public education with a terminal occupational emphasis should be a current goal.

6. Beyond initial preparation for employment, many, out of choice or necessity, will want to bolster an upward occupational climb with part-time and sometimes full-time courses and programs as adults. These should be available as part of the regular public school system. They should not be limited to a few high-demand and low-cost trades, but should provide a range of occupational choice as wide as those available to students preparing for initial entry.

7. Any occupation which contributes to the good of society is a fit subject for vocational education. In the allocation of scarce resources, first attention must be paid to those occupations which offer expanding opportunities for employment. In the elementary and junior high schools, attention can be paid only to groups of occupations which employ large numbers of people, and instruction must be restricted to broad principles, common skills, and pervasive attitudes which will be useful in a broad range of employment. These restrictions are less and less valid as the student goes through high school and junior college, until, in adult education, instruction is justified in even the most restricted field if it is valuable to the individual and to society.

8. Occupational preparation need not and should not be limited to the classroom, to the school shop, or to the laboratory. Many arguments favor training on the job. Expensive equipment need not be duplicated. Familiarization with the

environment and discipline of the workplace is an important part of occupational preparation, yet is difficult to simulate in a classroom. Supervisors and other employees can double as instructors. The trainee learns by earning. On the other hand, the employer and his supervisors may be more production than training oriented. The operations and equipment of a particular employer may cover only part of a needed range of skills, necessitating transfer among employers for adequate training. The ideal is to meld the advantages of institutional and on-the-job training in formal cooperative work-study programs.

9.   Effective occupational preparation is impossible if the school feels that its obligation ends when the student graduates. The school, therefore, must work with employers to build a bridge between school and work. Placing the student on a job and following up his successes and failures provides the best possible information to the school on its own strengths and weaknesses.

10.   No matter how good the system of initial preparation and the opportunities for upgrading on the job, there will always be need for remedial programs. Remedial programs will differ from the preventive in that many of the students will require financial assistance while in training; the courses must be closely oriented to the labor market to assure a quick return to employment; and the trainee will be impatient of what may seem to be the "frills" of regular vocational programs.

A System of Employment Education in the Ghetto*

In essence, a program to prepare ghetto youth adequately for employment differs in only two ways from a program with similar objectives for all youth: (1) though aiming at the same goals, it must start from further behind, and (2) it is of higher priority.

---

*Author's Note: In the thoughts expressed in this section, the author has been greatly influenced by the views and writings of Marvin J. Feldman.

When one lists the attributes which make a worker employable, he finds job skills low in the arrangement of priorities, which includes mental and physical health, a conviction that work is inherently good and is the most appropriate source of income, good work habits and the acceptance of discipline, the basic skills of communication and computation, a knowledge of the fundamentals of science and technology, and the knowledge and ability to make a wise vocational choice. Only the last three are ordinarily considered to be responsibilites of the educational system and the last is rarely provided. For the ghetto youth, none of these attributes can be assumed. Given public education's customary assignment of compensating for the failure of other aspects of society, programs encouraging these attributes must be built into the school curriculum and youth encouraged to remain there long enough to obtain the necessary preparation. Fortunately, there is evidence that where these relevant attributes are made available, retention is also improved.

Educators have been reluctant to place primary emphasis on the preparation for employment, fearing that it would thwart the more general goals of education for "life," usually meaning citizenship, culture, social skills, and pursuit of learning for learning's sake. Preparing ghetto youth for employment seems to find more ready acceptance because it is assumed that they are not likely to achieve the other goals. The dichotomy between employability and academic goals has arisen from the tendency to think of only specific job skills as the necessary requirement for employment. Listing the other and more critical requirements of employability should make it clear that no such dichotomy exists. The goals of education are difficult to define, but they include knowledge and the understanding of society and of one's self in relation to society, the ability to accumulate and process information and to make rational decisions based upon it, the identification and development of one's talents as a productive member of society, and a positive start in developing one's own life values. Nothing about preparing oneself for effective labor market participation need conflict with these broader goals, though conflict certainly can occur if preparation for employment is not pursued within an appropriate framework.

It is particularly necessary that the temptation be avoided to prepare the disadvantaged for only minimum participation in society and in the world of work. The goal must be to take them from where they are, overcoming their handicaps, to wherever they have the potential and develop the desire to go. Since most members of society find their highest achievement in their vocational activity (including homemaking), preparation for employment is critical not only to income and living standards but also to prestige, status, and self-esteem as well. In fact, as the following pages will indicate, vocational education as the core of the total curriculum may, for many, provide greater motivation and more academic achievement than might be possible in its absence.

1.   The Elementary School and the World of Work

Though studies have yet to credit a few brief summertime Head Start courses over four years with any major breakthrough in the education of the poor, one need only to look to the rapidly rising preschool enrollments of the children of the more affluent to know that early childhood education has much to offer.

Fundamentally, the elementary school has as its objective the provision of the basic knowledge and skills which are considered the minimum requirements of all members of society and which can develop the intellectual and social habits necessary for further acquisition and use of knowledge and for effective human relations.

Probably because the elementary schools are so firmly committed to preparing children for subsequent stages of schooling, the spoken and written word is both the substance and the technique of this instruction. Whether this is the only or the best way of transmitting such knowledge or building such habits in every child is rarely questioned. For the middle-class child, acquainted with the printed word and accustomed to oral communication by middle-class parents trained by the same pedagogical methods, no serious obstacle is presented, though many might learn better if taught by some other technique. For the ghetto product of poorly educated parents and broken homes, the customary techniques are unlikely to be satisfactory.[3] It may well be that most learn better by observation and by experience. For the "culturally deprived"[4] there is little alternative.

Employment orientation may make two contributions at this stage. Few would advocate teaching job skills to six to twelve-year olds. However, vocational education's techniques of learning by doing are most like the natural processes by which learning occurs in the preschool years. For the ghetto child particularly, there is need to give him the essential knowledge his home and neighborhood may not supply. He should have some awareness that (1) work as an employee, employer, or self-employed will be the primary source of income and determinant of family income for most people throughout their lives; (2) the range of employment opportunities is vast, each with its own requirements for preparation and access and each with its differing rewards; and (3) not now but at some point in the future a vocational choice must be made and preparation undertaken. The discovery of talents and their relation to the adult world of work and achievement and the gradual exposure to the choice between abstract approaches to learning and the manipulation of real objects can be aided by role playing and field trips related to the workings of the economic system and the labor market. Identification of learning styles, especially if nonverbal, and the opportunity to learn through the preferred style can limit failures, increase self-confidence, and lay a firmer foundation for later learning.

These are not untried theories, though experience is too

limited to draw more than the broad outlines of the approach. The Technology for Children program in the ghettos of Newark, New Jersey, and a similar program for middle-class children in the Nova schools in Fort Lauderdale, Florida, are examples worthy of examination.[5]

2. Occupational Education in the Junior High

By early adolescence, youth is beginning to yearn for participation in an adult world, and the visible relevance of schooling to that world and to his conceived goals are becoming critically important. To the committed college-bound youth, the curriculum of most junior highs is clearly relevant. The content of such curricula will help him meet the high school requirements which in turn will prepare him for college. For the noncollege-bound and particularly the disadvantaged youth, the relevance, though present, is difficult to identify. Most dropouts which occur in high school are probably foreordained when these students are in junior high and elementary schools, if not before. A curriculum will have a better chance of encouraging retention if it exposes all students to the workings of the economic and industrial system and to the full range of occupational choices which that system will offer him, and if it ties the academic content directly to preparation for those opportunities.

3. Education for Employment in the High School

At the time the older adolescent's interests are broadening to encompass the full range of adult experiences, the schools are convinced he should narrow his focus to the subject matter of specific disciplines taught under circumstances and by techniques as far removed from reality as possible. In the typical ghetto school, formal or informal tracking systems make apparent those who are destined for success or failure by the teachers' definitions. A relative few have the discipline and parental support to endure the college preparatory course with its singleness of purpose. Those being prepared for the manual trades find greater relevance in what they are doing. However, for minority youngsters, the chances are that they are either preparing for jobs which will occur where they cannot live or to which their access will be limited or, more realistically, for jobs which will keep them on the edge of poverty throughout their lives. Girls preparing for office occupations will probably fare best, but most employers still prefer the white suburban import. Reasons for continuing in the general track are not obvious to anyone. Each track tends to close off other alternatives. The notion of taking the ghetto youth from where misfortune has placed him, making opportunity believable to him, and taking him as far as he has the ability and can develop the ambition to go, is contrary to the system.

This stage of life is the time for integrating knowledge, for understanding a complex society, and for preparing to take part in its realities, not for compartmentalized disciplines. Though the word may be overworked, relevance is the key.[6] And to most students nothing is more relevant than how to make a living. The school's responsibilities, particularly in the ghetto, are: (1) to identify those areas of knowledge and understanding that society's experience have shown necessary for effective participation, (2) to find ways of presenting that material which will make its relevance apparent to the student, (3) to offer him the success experiences that will give him confidence that he too can absorb the necessary and relevant learning, (4) to insure that at whatever stage he chooses to leave the school system he will take with him something salable in the labor markets relevant to him, (5) to deliver on the promise that the educational system will never reject him though he may reject the system, and (6) to keep open numerous education and employment options beyond the high school.

Difficult as this multiple assignment may be, experiments such as the Richmond Plan in the San Francisco Bay Area schools, the Nova schools in Florida, the American Industries project in Wisconsin, the Partnership Vocational Education project in Michigan, the "zero-reject" concept in certain California schools, and others, have not only indicated the practicality of these objectives but also have provided insights into how they are to be attained.[7]

The common notion in each of these experiments goes beyond the rejection of the historical separateness of academic and vocational education. It takes occupational preparation rather than academic education as the core curriculum. It then uses the obvious relevance of this objective as a motivating factor, providing all of the desired academic knowledge but tying it directly to a goal to which the student can relate. An example (though by no means a perfect one nor the only model) is taken from the Pre-Tech Engineering program, an application of the Ford Foundation-funded Richmond Plan:[8] A team of teachers shepherding a group of some fifty normally-endowed but undermotivated youth plan a several weeks' project. The industrial arts instructor proposes construction of a device which will involve some woodworking, some metal work, some glass bending, and some electronics. The math instructor conceives a curriculum built around the project, as does the physics instructor. The English instructor will have the students write technical reports and perhaps read science fiction. Employers will find high school graduates available with a wide range of useful skills ready to be trained more specifically on the job. Junior colleges will find that their entrance requirements have been met (though many of the latter might well be questioned).

These examples are not the whole answer but they do provide a beginning. If the school truly accepts as its responsibility the discovery and development of individual talents, ways must be found to shape the offering to individual need. With proper development of attitude in elementary and junior high schools, that way may be the core curriculum approach. For those requiring a more specific goal it may be a vocational course in a specific skill. For others more anxious to enter the labor market, the answer may lie in a cooperative educational arrangement in which the student spends part of the time on campus and the remainder on a job (with the supervision provided by the school, so that the total is a related learning as well as an earning experience). The essentials are: (1) that the process start from where the student is by identifying what he has experienced and learned; (2) that it isolate what he needs to know; (3) that it discover ways of transmitting that knowledge in order to make its relevance clear; and (4) that as long as the student is willing to work toward some goal, no matter how modest that goal or his abilities, the system not reject him.

4.   The Postsecondary Stage

Though it is important in earlier stages to hold open as many alternatives as possible, all of the desired options cannot be described. Lack of education is an obstacle to employment, not only because it may deprive one of needed knowledge, but also because of the competitive handicaps involved. Such is the American faith in education that as long as an employer can hire a person with more education, regardless of its direct job relatedness, he is likely to do so. Unskilled and semiskilled jobs and entry levels of skilled jobs to be pursued through apprenticeship or on-the-job training will remain the route for most for some time. However, the trend is clearly toward formal postsecondary education, and those without it will soon be as competitively disadvantaged as those currently without a high school diploma.

What must be recognized is the beginning of a new stage of economic life in which human resources are the critical ones and in which one's formal education and training are the primary determinants of his income and status. A school system which once offered a modicum of the three R's to the population as citizens of a democracy, then selected out the relatively few needed to fill the demands for skilled workers and the even smaller number needed for professional positions, must now emphasize the employment needs of the individual and then relate these needs to the demands of the labor market.

This suggests a new goal for postsecondary institutions. Traditionally, the emphasis has been on selectivity, requiring the applicant to meet the institution's ambitious criteria. Now the emphasis must be on the individual's needs and what the institution can offer to help him fulfill his potential and achieve his goals.

Needed within easy commuting distance of everyone, and especially the ghetto resident, is an institution that combines the first two years of a four-year college course, associate degree programs in technical skills, two-year vocational training in skilled occupations, and short-term remedial courses preparing the disadvantaged for entry level jobs. In practice, it has proven necessary—because of the exalted ambitions of postsecondary schools—to build separate skill centers to provide adult basic education, prevocational orientation, and skill training for the disadvantaged. However, this again cuts the enrollee off from the mainstream and limits his upward mobility. The pride and motivation of attending a technical college as opposed to a Manpower Development and Training Act (MDTA) skill center should not be ignored. A great deal has been learned in recent years from MDTA and other manpower programs about specialized techniques for educating and training those from disadvantaged backgrounds. Unfortunately, there has been little transfer of these lessons to regular educational institutions.[9]

The postsecondary institution (and the secondary as well) should accept the obligation of placing the school dropout in his next job or on the next step of his career ladder. Nothing could provide the school with a more direct test of its performance than testing the quality of its product in the actual marketplace.

How to Get It Done

Most proposals for solving social and economic problems are conspicuous for their demands upon the public budgets. This is appropriate, for budgets represent our ordering of priorities and our allocation of resources. However, more efficient use of existing resources is always an alternative, and misguided use of increased funds is not always a contribution. The nation's slums do not receive their fair share of total education expenditures. "Impacted areas" federal aid to school districts already blessed with federal employment is more popular with Congress than Elementary and Secondary Education Act help for less prosperous schools. Congress has given more attention to remedial programs after the damage has been done than to preventing employment handicaps (though this appears to be changing).

However, it is those dollars which are available in the ghetto which are most likely to be spent inefficiently. The suburban school has a clear charter: "Get our kids into college." Though many are not well served by this objective, it does fit the majority. There is no clear objective for ghetto schools. An immediate contribution could be made by achieving greater effectiveness from dollars already being spent. As the specific objective of ghetto education from preschool through postsecondary, the preparation of every student for employment at the highest desired level attainable by him is a way to achieve that increased efficiency. A better job can always be done for more money, but there is nothing inherent in the approaches recommended which would raise costs per student. Neither is there anything in the proposals which would condemn the students to second-class economic or social citizenship. Whether achieved through organizations of community leaders, business groups, interested citizens, or parents, the design of a specific program tailored to community needs and a campaign to sell the notion to the decision-makers, operators, and customers of the schools could contribute more than lobbying for increased funds, desirable as the latter might be.

However, other avenues of help are available. Private business firms in their newly awakened interest in solving social problems have, in a few places, turned their attention to the schools. In Michigan, an automobile manufacturer and a public utility have each adopted a high school, seeking to aid the administrators, teachers, and students with advice, political support, access to equipment, and direct ties to employment opportunities. In Ohio, two other national firms have linked with vocational educators to provide special training institutions for school dropouts. Firms selling programmed and computer-aided education have proposed systems for ghetto as well as middle-class schools. The adoptive firms appear to have no clear objective in mind other than to "do good" and no plan for doing it. The Ohio effort is remedial rather than preventive in orientation. The vendors are primarily interested in selling their programs and devices. All are to be commended but need to clarify their objectives and promote a specific approach.

Demands for more community control of schools are heard sympathetically for many reasons, but the result is limited because the parents do not know what they want or how to get it. They know only that their children deserve a better deal. Yet public educators, by and large, react to signals from the tax-paying public. For the most part they are currently responding to the signals from the past when school was a "selecting out" process and from the vocal parents of the college-bound. But new voices are beginning to be heard. The new constituency must learn what it wants and how to make those wants known.

Important federal financial assistance was promised by the 1968 amendments to the Vocational Education Act, but that promise like many others remains to be fulfilled. The act sought in 1963 to end vocational education's nearly fifty-year concentration on specialized skill needs and to reorient the objectives to the employment needs of various population groups.

Specifically it sought greater assistance for "those whose academic and socio-economic handicaps make it difficult to profit from regular vocational education courses." When such advocacy brought little change, Congress took a more decisive stand with the 1968 amendments. Fifteen per cent of allotments to the states under the act were to be spent for the academic and socio-economically handicapped (or "special needs") group, to be supplemented by 25 per cent of all increases in allotments in subsequent years. A similar earmarking was assigned to increase postsecondary training. Ten per cent was to go to the physically and mentally handicapped.

The definition of vocational education was broadened to cover any education or training activity directly related to the preparation for employment. The use of the "special needs" funds and another category for "exemplary" (experimental and demonstration projects to reduce youth unemployment) projects was liberalized until they could be used to provide elementary schools with orientation to the world of work and year-by-year nurturing of the information and attitudes necessary for valid occupational choice. Priorities in all aspects of the program were to be given to locations with high incidence of unemployment and poverty. The physically and mentally handicapped are not primarily ghetto residents, but they are over-represented there. Home economics training was partially reoriented to provide consumer education and homemaker training to poor adults. Specific funds were authorized for cooperative programs joining the schools and the employer in the student's behalf, work-study programs to help students work their way through school, and residential schools.

Passage of the 1968 amendments came too late to affect the 1969 budget and vocational education and was a part of the 1970 veto battle over the congressional enlargement of the administration's education requests.

The table gives the authorizations for the fiscal years from 1969–73 and the actual appropriations for the fiscal year of

Programs, Authorizations and Appropriations
Under the Vocational Education Amendments of 1968

(For the Fiscal Year in Millions of Dollars)

Program	Authorizations					Appropriations
	1969	1970	1971	1972	1973	1970
Comprehensive state programs						
Grants to states	319.5	508.5	607.5	607.5	508.5	307.5
Additional programs for disadvantaged persons	40.0	40.0	—	—	—	17.0
Activities of National Advisory Council	0.10	0.15	0.15	0.15	—	.2
Administration of state plans and activities of state advisory councils	Such sums as Congress may appropriate					2.4
Planning & evaluation						.9
Research and training (State Research Coordinating Units)	35.5	56.5	67.5	67.5	56.5	1.1
Exemplary programs	15.0	57.5	75.0	75.0	—	13.0
Residential vocational schools						
Demonstration schools	25.0	30.0	35.0	35.0		—
Grants to states	15.0	15.0	—	—		—
Subsidy for interest payments by states	5.0	10.0	—	—		—
Consumer and homemaking education	—	25.0	35.0	50.0	—	15.0
Cooperative programs	20.0	35.0	50.0	75.0		14.0
Work-study programs	35.0	35.0	—	—		4.3
Curriculum development	7.0	10.0	—	—		.9
Training of vocational education personnel	25.0	10.0				5.7
Administration of new programs	Such sums as Congress may appropriate					—

1970. The Administration has recommended a $20 million increase for 1971 while the Senate and House would both move from the 1970's $380 million total to the neighborhood of $440 million, still little more than half of the total authorization. But the way the money is spent may make more differences than the amount available. The additional state grant funds can be used in the same old way for the same old purpose, but not for the same people and in the same places because of the earmarking for the disadvantaged, the handicapped and postsecondary education. The funds can also be used by committed state and local vocational educators (prodded by interested and organized citizens) to begin or to supplement the process of preventive preparation for employment. In addition, in research and training, in exemplary programs, in the residential school provisions, in homemaking and consumer education, and in the work-study section, there are funds available to the Commissioner of Education for special grants to aggressive and innovative states over and above those provided by the formula allotments of the basic program. Various levels of vigor are found among the states but can be stimulated by well-organized pressure. More often than not, it is the academic rather than the vocational educators who have to be persuaded that employment preparation is the appropriate core.

National and state vocational education advisory councils were established by the 1968 Act in the hope of bringing to bear independent pressure within the system. Whether they will be independent in fact and take a broad and constructive view remains to be seen. Other concerned citizens, perhaps acting through Chambers of Commerce, the National Alliance of Businessmen, or the Urban Coalition could provide the necessary force for change. Such groups have shown interest in vocational education in the past but have never understood the system or the needs of youth well enough to have a specific program to promote. The primary result of such unfocused efforts is usually more of the same.

Business groups should have particular interest in an approach by which they live but which has never been attempted in public education: reward for performance. Public schools are financed on the basis of input, but competition from private sources or from a system designed to pay for results might bring interesting changes. Such a reward system might produce its own innovation. Short of that, much innovation will occur from dedicated people within the system, but acceleration of change will require enlightened and persistent community, business, and public demand.

Any long-range solution to the employment and earning problems of ghetto youth (and the adults they will become) must encompass major reorientation in the way they are prepared for work. Few American youth are well prepared for employment by the schools, but most have enough other advantages going for them. Those deprived by family and community background of such supplementary assistance need special help from the schools.

The key is to adopt the clear objective of preparation for employment as the central focus and relate all other education activities to it. A corollary of that focus is an individualized approach committed to taking each youth from where he is as far as he can and wants to go. Preparation merely for entry level skills in a secondary labor market will bring neither economic nor social progress over current conditions. The assumption, unproven though it is, must be that ghetto youth have the full potential of any other group in the society but merely start further behind. They must be prepared to compete for a higher education and for those jobs which offer the most and best opportunities, particularly in the central cities. Innovative techniques for achieving this objective are in the advanced stages of experimentation. They are fragmented, scattered, and promoted by no coherent force. Without that organized support their spread will be slow while the need remains critical.

3. Seven Strategies for Success in Vocational Education

Seymour L. Wolfbein

This paper asks and attempts to answer the following question: What are the specific strategies which yield the best promise for endowing disadvantaged persons in the urban centers with what is needed to move them into gainful employment through vocational education?

Specific recommendations and programs are offered in this paper; and if these are to be successful, they require the presence of a favorable environment. Certain of the required conditions, which are set forth in the first section of this paper, would have been regarded as revolutionary so recently as a decade ago; today they have become part of the conventional wisdom. This is fine so far as it goes. But the catch is that though these conditions are now honored in theory, they are often grudgingly accepted in practice, even ignored or deliberately fought. And unless they are present, no educational endeavor can successfully surmount the many problems involved and achieve the goal of opening the American world of work to the uneducated, the unskilled, and the unwanted.

Before moving on to the discussion of these necessary conditions, the author would first like to make clear that there are two issues that he has purposely avoided or underplayed.

The first is the alleged "low status" and "low dignity" of

vocational education. To describe vocational education thus is merely to define the problem in terms of the problem itself. The statement is tautological, and furthermore it strikes at symptoms rather than root causes. Practically all of those who have successfully pursued a vocational curriculum and are now gainfully occupied in a related endeavor think highly of vocational education; those who have been unsuccessful think the contrary. The same situation, of course, exists in other fields of study and work. In any event, the phrases "low dignity" and "low status" are culture-colored terms out of the white-collar vocabulary.

The second issue given light treatment in this paper is the need in vocational education for the most up-to-date techniques and equipment. But where else isn't there such a need? And is this really at the cutting edge of the problem in vocational education? Indeed, it has yet to be proven that the educational and training methods and materials in vocational education are in fact less up to date than those used, say, in teaching grammar or French or sociology. In view of the developments in vocational education during the 1960's, there must now be innumerable installations of a technically advanced nature. At any rate, the results of poor concepts and methods in vocational education are often remedied by retraining efforts, including on-the-job training. Again, the same pattern holds true in other fields; poor academic training is often remedied in college or on the job. No matter what the field, remediation may not be successful or may not even occur, and poor workmanship and mediocre careers are often the consequence.

General Principles

There are three basic conditions that must be present if vocational education programs are to be successful.

1. *The opportunity for vocational education must be offered in an environment completely free of discrimination among its clients.*

Such an environment must be provided not only for the central-city blacks, but also for Irish Catholics in South Boston and Hasidic Jews in Brooklyn, as well as for the millions of Puerto Rican and Mexican-American slum dwellers throughout urban America.

Clearly, it is essential that discrimination must be eliminated throughout the entire range of educational endeavors, but nowhere is this more important than in the case of vocational education. The economic, educational, and training deficits among the urban poor, unemployed, and disadvantaged must be overcome before civil liberties can become a viable concept in our society. And at this particular juncture, vocational education has the potential means, immediacy, and responsiveness to help bring this about. This, in fact, is the *raison d'etre* for this paper. This view is premised on the enormous range as well as variety of present vocational education curricula, together with the rising employment prospects available to those who are successful in their engagement with them.

For those who have studied and practiced in this area, this is indeed a fascinating turn of events in vocational education. Gordon Swanson, noting some of the recent federal legislation on behalf of vocational education, has observed:

> Taken together, this package of legislation may be regarded as a massive social protest movement. Indeed it may be the largest and most widespread social protest movement in the United States within the last hundred years. Like the Morrill Act which generated land-grant universities, the present package of legislation may generate a new framework within which institutions can deal with the problems provoking the protest. . . . The social protest contained within current legislation is not unrelated to this earlier mandate directed at economic opportunity and vocational education . . . A significant number of people are not participating fully in the economic life of the nation . . . The current vocational emphasis may be a reaction to a con-

tinuing conflict regarding the time needed to train for various occupations or skills.[1]

It should be noted that nondiscrimination is treated here as a general principle and not as a specific strategy. A reason for this is that education and training, including vocational education, cannot carry the ball alone. Each educational discipline may be free of discrimination in its own practices, but it may still founder because of the discrimination prevailing in the world of work—a situation resulting in part through the feedback received by those embarking on training courses. This can have the most serious consequences to attitudes and performance, as those who participated in "stay-in-school" campaigns are aware. Every study conducted during the 1960's on the contrasting experiences in the labor force of high school dropouts versus graduates showed that, while in general the unemployment rate for dropouts is higher than the one for those who persevere to diploma time, the unemployment rate for *nonwhite graduates* is higher than that for *white dropouts*—and the nonwhites know it.

2. *Vocational education and training opportunity can be undertaken by everyone.*

The first general proposition holds that everyone should have the opportunity to engage in this field; the second holds that, without exception, everyone can take advantage of that opportunity; i.e., has the ability to do so, and can be guided and counseled and motivated to do so.

This principle comes up against some strongly entrenched views, the following being an excellent example:

Our economy just doesn't have any jobs for certain types of people. If it continues to develop along its present course, the number of such unemployables seems likely to grow rather rapidly . . . for the assortment of jobs which need to be done is simply out of kilter with the natural distribution of brains . . . we have apparently built ourselves unintentionally and without quite realizing it, a society which calls for a distribution of intelligence entirely different from which God provided. It remains to be seen whether we can make it work.[2]

This statement by a distinguished writer, John Fischer, summarizes a widely held view, as anyone who has tried to launch training programs in slum areas knows. It conjures up a picture of the immutability of the sacred IQ as measured by currently used instruments, a procedure fortunately now being challenged. It disregards research and documentation of the impact of social and economic conditions on the measurement of IQ; e.g., that IQ declines with the number of household moves made by the families of school children in urban areas. It even opposes the philosophy of Binet, who held in 1909 that "one increases that which constitutes the intelligence of a school child, namely, the capacity to learn, to improve with instruction." It flies in the face of some of the most successful retraining programs of the 1960's, in which mental retardates were successfully trained for a wide variety of jobs. Its economics are all wrong in view of the prospective kind of changes in the occupational structure; the relatively high rates of growth in the ranks of surgeons, vocational educators, and other occupations do not all necessarily require similar degrees of skill and talent.

The hard, cold truth of the matter is that this stated purpose apparently cannot be achieved, for the new skills lie almost exclusively in the technical and semitechnical fields. A substantial educational background is required before an individual can be trained for such jobs. In addition, the individual must have certain aptitudes, the motivation to undertake rigorous and difficult training, and then be willing to move to an area of the country where such a skill is required.[3]

This statement, representing the minority views in the House of Representatives regarding the Manpower Development and Training Act of 1962, reflects the view that trainees have neither the educational attainments for moving into vocational training nor the required attitudes and motivations to consummate the training. As it so happened, the first year of operations under this act indeed seemed to confirm this view; only 3 per cent of the trainees had less than an eighth-grade education even though people with such limited school attainment made up 20 per cent of all the unemployed. But then it was found that the test being used by the employment services to screen potential trainees actually screened them *out* with enormous proficiency. Thereupon, new testing procedures were devised that screened *in*—with excellent predictive results— many of the disadvantaged, whose aversion to paper and pencil tests had nothing to do with their training and work potential but rather with prior encounters and inability to cope with words and ideas outside their culture.

The House minority statement, however, is perfectly correct in pointing out that some educational background is required of those taking vocational training. After one year of operation, the provision of basic training in reading, writing, and numbers skills was embodied in an amendment to the Manpower Act—and this, again, is a necessary condition for successful strategies in this arena.

The statement also expresses one of the most prevalent attitudes regarding trainees in the vocational field; i.e., their assumed lack of motivation and willingness to undertake, persevere in, and follow up on their training. This is not the place to engage in an extensive discussion of the complex human attributes involved, but it should be pointed out that aspirations and motivations are a critical problem in this field and that it is fatal to overlook that problem. Lack of motivation stems largely from a lack of sufficient, varied, meaningful, and successful encounters with the environment that is typically experienced by the urban disadvantaged. Nevertheless, there is enough experience now indicating that these traumas can be overcome if enough resources are devoted to contending with the problem, and especially if programs are individually oriented. It has been found that motivation takes some surprising turns if, for example, the two missing front teeth are replaced, or in another a training stipend is provided, or an indigenous trainer is used, or a friend actually gets a job after training, or a pair of shoes is provided, and so forth.

Perhaps the most noteworthy finding of the past decade's experimental and demonstration programs in vocational training has been the understanding that the urban poor, unemployed, blacks, whites, youthful offenders, armed forces rejectees, and all others who are categorized invidiously have as wide a spectrum of interests, aptitudes, motivations, and talents as any other groups.

Lowell A. Burkett, executive director of the American Vocational Association, commenting on the 1968 amendments to the Vocational Educational Act of 1963, underscored the use of the word "access" in the legislation, which calls for the provision of vocational educational opportunity so that all "will have ready access to vocational training or retraining which is of high quality." Burkett further states that "the key word 'access' also has social implications, for vocational education is in reality a social movement. It is an educational process that, by its very nature, promotes democracy. It builds on each student's abilities and aspirations. And it is an avenue of opportunity for all who seek to become productive workers—without regard to race, creed, class, or national origin."[4]

3. *Vocational education and training opportunity must be coordinated with "first chance" and "second chance" institutions, which also means coordination between the programs available through both public and private sectors.*

Education as used in this paper is taken to mean the first round of learning experience; it can vary in length from less than a grade school education to a post baccalaureate degree. Training includes all future transactions with the learning process, whether it be undertaken to complete what was left unfinished in the first round or to update what was achieved previously.

Education, as so defined, can be as academically abstract as a sequence in topology or as deliberately oriented vocationally as a course in arc welding. Training can be as specifically skill-oriented as a course in licensed practical nursing or as basic as learning to read and write—which, in fact, takes place under the Manpower Act, as already indicated.

There is no intention here to present any new concepts but simply to make clear that if vocational education is going to make its hoped for impact on the urban disadvantaged, two conditions will have to be present. First, both educational processes must contain a mixture of the academic and vocational. In other words, the first formal round of learning must have as much work-oriented curricula and subsequent rounds of learning must have as much academic curricula as are needed by the clients. Second, the relationship between the two processes of education should not be merely sequential. We must begin to break down those artificial barriers between the two which now require (often by law) that a person make the try (and fail) in a formal high school setting before being permitted to move into training programs. A classic case in point is the recent announcement by the Department of Labor cutting back the Neighborhood Youth Corps program for out-of-school youth in order "not to encourage dropouts."

Closely related to these points is the one emphasizing the importance of involving the private sector. As used here, the term "private sector" means all employing institutions that can offer training or employment opportunities and therefore includes nonprofit institutions as well as the activities of government agencies in this field. The impact of federally-financed programs has clearly demonstrated the increased participation, the increased training completions, and the increased job placement and duration of employment that are possible with such activities as on-the-job training. It should be pointed out that these programs are often coupled with academic training, either on or off the job site.

Three other points should be made briefly, if only in recognition of their overriding importance. Again, these apply to all educational endeavors but have a particularly vital significance for the vocational education field in particular. All three are matters of over-all national policy.

First is the need for a continuation of an active *economic policy* nationally involving a commitment to employ all fiscal and monetary instruments to ensure a level and rate of economic growth that in turn will ensure the needed job opportunities for all who seek them. All bets are off, particularly for the urban disadvantaged youth, if we fail on this one.

Second is the need for a continuation of an active *manpower policy* nationally involving a commitment to maximize the educational and training opportunities for all who need them under conditions of fair standards and without discrimination. The legislation on vocational education during the past half-dozen years fulfills these requirements, although it still remains to be seen whether sufficient resources will be made available to make the provisions truly come alive.

Third is the need for new developments in a *work-incomes policy* nationally that would provide a level of family income permitting youth to enter into and continue in the education-training process. The key is to remove finances as the barrier to the completion of an education—training sequence needed by an individual, whatever that sequence may be.

Specific Strategies

Of all the myths about vocational education, perhaps the most burdensome is the view that it is the educational no man's land in America. Not only is this hurtful, because it affects the clients negatively even before they enter into vocational education, but it is also wrong. The fact of the matter is that vocational education has been extremely successful in a number of its enterprises.

Vocational education is a term that encompasses a wide variety of endeavors. This includes, for instance, home economics which is job related to relatively few of its enrollees (although its potential for helping the urban disadvantaged in other roles is enormous) and agriculture which only recently has emerged with responsive programs in the business sense. Also included are critically important areas such as health, trade, and industrial occupations, as well as technical, distributive, and office occupations; the last two in particular providing significant numbers of workers in fields where there is an urgent labor shortage. Enrollments in federally-aided vocational education classes increased from a total of 4.2 million in the fiscal year of 1963 to an estimated 8.2 million in the fiscal year of 1968. Of these, secondary school enrollments rose from about 2.0 million to 4.2 million during the same period of time.

From a job-market point of view, perhaps the most successful program has been that in the office occupation field. For example, just between the fiscal years 1964 and 1966, secondary school vocational education enrollments rose by 1.5 million. Most of this increase occurred in just one field—office occupations—which accounted for 1.25 million of the upturn. Almost all the remainder were in the trade and industrial category.

Why office occupations? They respond, of course, to an insatiable demand. The number of secretaries, stenographers, and typists employed in this country rose by an almost unbelievable one million just in the decade 1958–68, and Department of Labor projections to 1975 indicate that there will be 215,000 job openings for these occupations *each year*. The entry jobs are also clear cut, their demands definable; the skills involved are long established and subject to relatively little change. One can peel off at different levels, relating education to entry jobs; e.g., one can stop at typing or go on for the stenographer rung. Cooperative work arrangements are relatively easy to get and the jobs are mainly in the white-collar world; the teachers have a college education and are peers with the guidance counselors who "understand" the jobs involved. All of this hardly describes an educational wasteland. In fact, there would appear to be present most of the overt signs of success in the conventional sense of secondary education.

At any rate, an examination of successful programs—as well as of others not quite so successful—suggests certain specific strategies that are needed for responsive programs that will aid the urban disadvantaged in moving into a positive role in the world of work. Seven such strategies are identified here. Each must be included in an over-all program in this field. Each is important in its own right, but even more important is their interaction. Strategy Number One—money—is obviously the root of beneficence; but it avails little without the other six strategies. Strategy Number Two—cooperative work programs —is critical; but it is really not going to catch fire without the others. Bringing to bear all of these strategies on the design of a program will make for a critical mass.

1.   Matching Resources with Needs

Recent legislative advances have resulted in substantial increases in funds for vocational education at the federal and state levels. While there is no gainsaying the significant rise in resources over all, the difficulty is that adequate funding is not necessarily going into the areas of greatest need. Most of the inner cities of the metropolitan areas of the country, where disproportionate concentrations of the disadvantaged poor live and go to school, still do not have the resources required to mount responsive programs. Cities such as Philadelphia are forced to refer applicants to catchall vocational programs rather than enroll them in the more adequately designed ones; because of a lack of funds there aren't enough places in these programs. Changing needs are not matched by changes in the supply of resources, and the first necessary step is to match the two properly.

In addition to all other considerations, there are two compelling arguments for increasing vocational education resources in these areas. The first point is the very obvious one that this is where the problem is concentrated. The second, though not so obvious, point is that the numbers involved are relatively small, even though the incidence or rate of unemployment and of poverty is very high among the disadvantaged urban residents. For example, nonwhite unemployed *of all ages* in 1968 in the 20 largest metropolitan areas of the United States numbered less than a quarter of a million. This represented a fraction of 1 per cent of the American labor force. The incidence of poverty is harshly high among black families in central cities. In terms of numbers, however, the number of black families that fell below the poverty line in 1968 was about 700,000 for *all* central cities in the United States, including family units comprising the elderly and others unlikely to avail themselves of any kind of education, vocational or otherwise. Insofar as the concentration of the problem is concerned, it should be noted that black families have relatively higher proportions of children of school age. In 1968, 35 per cent of all black central-city residents were five-to-nineteen years of age, about a third higher than the proportion of this age group among white residents.

Given the qualitative as well as the quantitative needs for this population group, it is difficult not to place first as a proposed strategy the immediate and deliberate allocation of the funds to do the job, considering the relative small requirements in the face of our total gross national product, personal income, labor force, and so forth.

2.   Expanding Cooperative Education

The amendments to the Vocational Education Act of 1963 authorize grants to assist states in expanding their cooperative vocational programs that relate on-the-job work experience to

classroom education. We will let the legislation speak for itself:
Through such programs, a meaningful work experience is combined with formal education, enabling students to acquire knowledge, skills, and appropriate attitudes. Such programs remove the artificial barriers which separate work and education and, by involving educators with employers, create interaction whereby the needs and problems of both are made known.[5]

Where cooperative work programs have been instituted, they have had enormously gratifying results. The practice has been a long-standing one, and has been widely known as "distributive education." By the middle of 1969, Distributive Education Clubs of America, made up exclusively of job-holding students, had close to 100,000 members.

These programs permit the use of the entire community as a preparatory laboratory for employment. Out-of-school training on the job is provided under the combined purview of the school and employing institution. Academic credit is given for the on-the-job training. Students are paid a fair wage for their work time as agreed by all the parties concerned, and the student thus gets the opportunity to run the gantlet of the actual job market; the employer in many instances gets work output as well as the first chance for the student's services when he or she makes an entry into full-time work.

While reports about ongoing programs are almost uniformly glowing, cooperative programs, however, are not generally easy to establish.[6] It takes qualified personnel to seek out employers with relevant opportunities, cooperation in establishing training opportunities, and most especially a willingness to provide these opportunities to urban disadvantaged youth. Union relations can be touchy. Both federal and state legislation regulating wages paid to workers over sixteen prohibit a student from displacing a regular full-time employee; these regulations also restrict employment of young people in certain fields, particularly in trade and industrial occupations.

The 1968 amendments are particularly important in this context since they provide additional funds for program coordinators and instructors in cooperative work programs, reimburse employers when necessary for added costs involved, pay for such extras as transportation costs for students, etc. These are absolutely vital if any significant number of the difficult-to-reach urban disadvantaged are to be involved.

The extension and expansion of cooperative work programs may well be the strategy deserving first priority among the various strategies designed to improve vocational education opportunity in the central cities as well as elsewhere in the country. It is difficult to think of anything else which would do more to reach the disadvantaged and facilitate their transition from school to work. Cooperative work programs are as vital to vocational education as teaching hospitals are to schools of medicine.

Cooperative work programs have analogs in a variety of training programs under the Manpower Development and Training Act and other legislation providing for "coupled" training, involving both classroom instruction and on-the-job training. These have proven to be some of the most successful retraining programs conducted under this legislation, two reasons being that they provide work-related remuneration while training and improve the prospect for job placement (with the cooperating employer). But a word of warning is needed. These programs tend to involve less of the disadvantaged since in many cases the "riskier" prospects are screened out. This, of course, negates a major aim of these programs and indicates, on the basis of past experience, that the road ahead will not be easy.

3. Individualizing the Format

One of the prime characteristics of the urban disadvantaged is the diversity of individual characteristics. In this category are men and women of different ages, color, family structure and background, interests, aptitudes, talents, goals, motivations, and length and variety of prior experience with the learning process. The statement may be obvious, but it needs underscoring because the literature in this field uses statistical generalizations in making its points. Hence the trade talk about "the Negro family," "the urban disadvantaged," "the American poor," "white and black children," and so forth. In confronting strategy and program, however, we must disaggregate—and this is really the point about this point. This is a critical proposition for all education, but again it is particularly critical for the vocational field and even more so for its clients among the urban disadvantaged.

A third strategy, therefore, calls for the development of a very flexible, individualized format for vocational education. The curricula of the various fields should be *paced* to the individual differentials of the clients, premised on the understanding that for significant numbers the training period may be relatively brief. With entry into the world of work relatively imminent, the testing of the individual in the realities of the job market will therefore come sooner than later. This means keeping an eye on every avenue of entry in every job field, with the training designed accordingly. It means that some will finish as keypunch operators, while others will proceed to programming and still others will go on to post high school work in information science. It means that some will finish as body repairmen or proceed to auto mechanic and diagnostic work, while others will go on to colleges of engineering technology. Or that some will finish as file clerks, while others will proceed to secretarial work or go on to colleges of business education. Likewise, while some will finish as hospital helpers, others will move on to licensed practical nursing and still others will go on to colleges of allied health programs.

Such a strategy calls for a creative approach. It requires the conceptualization of careers and the development of corresponding programs and curricula that have recognized terminal points along the way matching those in the world of work. This now exists in some areas of vocational education, and it has long existed in most professions. The key is to make this accessible to everyone in a recognized place and format, with clear identification of the prospects and potentials at every stage in the sequence. There must also be available nonvocational education courses for those able to move to advanced rungs on the career ladder. Such a sequenced and paced design will go far toward eliminating that decision, made about the ninth grade, which almost irrevocably commits students to compartmentalized courses of education.

What is proposed here for vocational education is really no different from the kind of experience that tens of thousands of young people encounter every year in the academic arena. Not everyone gets into medical school, even with a baccalaureate. Significant numbers of young people move off into some related career when they do not go on to law schools, colleges of education, or even college at all. Likewise, in the vocational area there will be many who will not necessarily go on to the magic land of the high school diploma—although that could change if we succeed in launching programs carrying out the strategies suggested here.

4. Eliminating Tests

One of the prime characteristics of the American school system is the free access that everyone has to public school through the twelfth grade—and, indeed, a person's presence is legally required. By "free" two important things are meant: Schooling is free of cost to the pupil—though the bill may go to the parents via taxation—and free of testing. Considering what happens later on in a person's scholastic career, especially if he wants to go on to what is known in the trade as an institution of higher learning, it is to be noted that we make a very important assumption about children who are five or six years of age. We assume that *every* child, including those children with the most intractably difficult mental and physical disabilities, gets a chance to encounter the formal learning process.

Tests, of course, are used for wide variety of purposes in the years from kindergarten through the twelfth grade for judging achievement, for grade placement, for pupil teaching, for guidance and counseling, and for a wide variety of other pupil assessment purposes. However, the pendulum swings to and fro, and now even the once sacrosanct IQ test is having a hard time, particularly in urban disadvantaged areas. Witness the recent (July 1969) action by the Los Angeles school system dropping such tests for new entrants on the grounds that they discriminate against Mexican-Americans and other minority groups.

The fourth strategy for vocational education has the virtue of eliminating substantive issues about tests—what kinds are better or best, how and when they are used and for what purposes, whether they should or can be "culture free," how predictive they are of what, and so forth. It is based on a simple premise:

Tests should not be used at all; that is to say, everyone wishing to enter the vocational education field while in school should be able to do so not only without cost but also without tests.

Without this kind of "free" access, it is difficult to see how it will be possible to bring about a significant impact on the problem of helping the urban disadvantaged in their transition from school to work through the medium of vocational education. If education is paced to the potential of the person, in accordance with our third strategy, the full range of tests, evaluations, and the like would be very much in order, *not* to screen out but rather to help in a continuous assessment of the best possible terminal points related to entry jobs in the world of work for a given individual. Each year tens of thousands of young people are screened not only out of the academic area but also out of a variety of vocational areas on the basis of their previous achievements in the grades. If vocational education is to be responsive to the needs of the people in the places where the greatest need exists, it must be viewed as an opportunity station for everyone within the formal educational system.

Nor should tests be used when an individual applies to a second-chance vocational program outside formal schooling; e.g., the training and retraining offered under manpower and related legislation. Those eligible for such programs, as a matter of public policy, are defined and described in the legislation. It is difficult to see why these people have to pass through testing screens any more than do children entering the public school system. Even if the matter of funds is a factor—and perhaps especially when it is—there is a serious question whether public policy is not actually being thwarted if a queue is set up on the basis of tests that "cream" the potential clientele or deliberately screen out the riskier cases. Again, if the vocational education component of manpower training and retraining is to be responsive to the needs of the people in the areas of greatest deprivation, then it must function as a second-chance institution for *everyone*.

Our fourth strategy in no wise demeans the importance of student assessment. Rather, taken together with the other strategies, it underscores its importance as a means of providing the needed intelligence for determining individual progress in a custom-tailored and paced program. It simply requires that the student assessment be done *after* the student gets into the program.

5.   Opening Opportunities for Continuous Education

Vocational education should be a continuous system, available to all those who need it whether they are in or out of school, whether they are in or out of the job market. To put this another way insofar as vocational education is concerned, certainly where the urban disadvantaged are involved, the word "dropout" ought to be dropped out of the lexicon of the trade. For example, the young man of seventeen who leaves after the tenth grade and takes a job for six months, whatever it may be, should be able to enter the vocational education system if he then wants or needs it. This should occur as a matter of course in a vocational education school center or a manpower training program, again with free access—and without any invidious labelling.

Such is the goal of our fifth strategy. The nub of this strategy lies in the development of a related set of vocational programs, operating in tandem in both the in-school and out-of-school settings. This is in contrast with the separately designed and compartmentalized systems now existing in most jurisdictions—to the further disadvantage of the urban disadvantaged.

Free and easy passage between the in-school and out-of-school settings would create a flexible system offering (a) a formal school setting for those who want and can pursue the curricula involved, including cooperative work programs; (b) out-of-school, on-the-job training for those who want and can pursue the curricula involved, including coupling with academic instruction as needed; and (c) an opportunity to move between the two for those who require this at different stages in their career and training development.

One of the groups most neglected by training and jobs programs for the urban disadvantaged are those who do get jobs but at the lowest levels of skill and pay. This group has a high level of unemployment, lives below the poverty level, and is characterized by a high rate of job turnover (often voluntary) because of the dead-end nature of the available work. Recent attempts to act on this problem at the federal level through the private sector illustrate clearly the need for the availability of continuous vocational education opportunity and the use of as many settings as possible in seeking solutions. The language used in describing the need for the recently established MA-5 JOBS program and its upgrading component point up some of the main directions suggested by the strategy under discussion (italics added):

> Upgrading refers to a *flexible program of occupational training conducted on or off the job site* to advance persons already employed to a job at a higher skill level. *Persons to be upgraded must be identified as working disadvantaged* unable to move beyond entry level positions, or must be persons upgraded to enter positions where there is a recognized shortage of skilled persons. Traditionally, industry has conducted a wide variety of training aimed at upgrading the skills of its existing work force. Access into upgrading training programs is usually either through a job bidding system allowing an employee a reasonable period of time to master a job of a higher level or through aptitude tests. *This type of selection process has left numbers of employees in entry level positions from which they are unable to advance due to their failure to pass the job bidding or aptitude test requirements.* The employer has considerable flexibility in *structuring the upgrading program for each enrollee.* The result of the upgrading program should be the occupational advancement of at least two skill levels above the skill level of the employee, and should also be reflected by at least a 10 per cent wage increase upon completion.

> Recent amendments to the Manpower Development and Training Act established priority in the use of Skill Centers operating under the direction of the U.S. Department of Health, Education and Welfare as a supplier of education services to manpower training programs. In order to carry out this provision of the Act, *each proposal must give full consideration to the use of Skill Center facilities for job related basic education* wherever possible.[7]

This kind of program uses a variety of the strategies suggested here including the provision of funds, the involvement of the private sector, the use of on-the-site training, access without tests, the extension of vocational education even into the world of work itself, and a crossover with skill centers.

6.   Providing Supportive Services

The MA-5 JOBS program with its upgrading activities also provides for the training of the unemployed hardcore. It is also of particular interest that, aside from the actual training costs, and related transportation and administrative costs for which employers are reimbursed, there are five program components which each training program is to provide and for which reimbursement is also made. These include:

Initial orientation and counseling—"Employee orientation in program objectives—proper work habits, cooperation with supervisor, personal grooming, payroll procedures— . . ."

Job related basic education—"Basic or remedial reading, writing, arithmetic, and communication skills required for job performance."

Special counseling and job coaching—"A mandatory component. Personal, individual assistance for in-plant, job-related activities and problems. May also include more comprehensive counseling relative to absences, tardiness, etc."

Medical and dental services—"Initial physical exams, minor medical and dental treatment and inexpensive prosthesis, such as glasses, teeth, and hearing aids."

Supervisory and human relations training—"Attitudinal training for supervisors and other regular employees who will be working with the new employee. This component is highly recommended for inclusion in the training program."

The very wording of these provisions—particularly those calling for special counseling and job coaching on a mandatory basis—reflects the hard experience of a half-dozen years or so, which have brought home the need for providing a wide variety of supportive services along with the substantive training where the more intractable among the hardcore disadvantaged are concerned. As training programs have reached increasingly out towards this group, legislation has correspondingly increased the provisions for the size and variety of supportive services. Although their availability is still far from adequate, the situation is better than that of most in-school programs.

The fact is that we are not about to make a real dent in the problem of employing the central-city hardcore through the provision of vocational education alone. We now have enough experience through experiment and demonstration to know that education and training are just one part of the very tightly interrelated web of activities that are required.[8] This strategy, therefore, has to do with the inimical environment encountered by the disadvantaged person outside the educational and training milieu, and it calls for building supportive services to help them contend with the very design of programs. But it should be noted that vocational education itself requires some vitally important supportive services from the over-all social environment—a basic condition for the success of education noted at the beginning of this paper.

7. Securing Better Teachers

The first of the following quotations is from the Kerner Commission report on civil disorders and is the first item proposed under the heading "Provision of Quality Education In Ghetto Schools." The second is from a report on a successful program in this field in New Haven, Connecticut, that is described in detail later in the next section. Both relate to our seventh and final strategy—the one that may turn out to be the most difficult of all to consummate even though it is the most obvious. Simply enough, we are dealing here with the great need for quality personnel in vocational education.

The teaching of disadvantaged children requires special skills and capabilities. Teachers possessing these qualifications are in short supply. We need a national effort to attract to the teaching profession well-qualified and highly motivated young people, and to equip them to work effectively with disadvantaged students ... Class work alone, however, cannot be expected adequately to equip future teachers of disadvantaged children. Intensive in-service training programs designed to bring teacher candidates into frequent and sustained contact with inner-city schools are required. Other professionals and non-professionals working in ghetto-related activities—social workers, street workers—could be included as instructors in teacher training programs.[9]

Staff members in each of these courses must have practical experience, theoretical knowledge, intellectual drive, possess a dynamic personality and express a *sincere willingness* to work with students not particularly motivated toward high school. These characteristics are difficult to find in every candidate, yet to compromise any one of these characteristics is to invite failure of the program. The kind of student attracted to these courses requires the very best teaching talent the school system can attract, for teachers in these courses serve as counselors, instructors, advisors, friends, private tutors in other subjects, arbitrators and an assortment of other "duties."[10]

All education needs quality teachers perhaps more now than at any other time in our history. Vocational education is already having great difficulty getting its share of qualified teachers and is expected to have even greater difficulty in the future when competition is keen all over. This could be aggravated by the harassments present in vocational education because of the clientele and places it serves, which make the grass in the other educational areas look much greener.

It need hardly be pointed out that nowhere in education are tensions more exacerbated than in the teacher-administration-community relationships of the urban metropolitan areas.

Ironically, the larger supply of teachers in some of the inner cities is now being generated in part by the policy of occupational deferments under current Selective Service practice. The Teacher Corps and some programs under the Education Professions Act are making a few, though relatively a very few, people available for this field. Some colleges of education are increasing their efforts in preparing teachers for work in the inner city. Yet the vocational education field itself is hardly unanimous in assessing the importance of a college degree to secondary school teachers in many of its curricula. All this throws into some doubt the operational effectiveness of attempting to make "sincere willingness" a prime attribute of the teacher working with the urban disadvantaged.

Two Case Studies

Considering the current state of disarray in educating and training the urban disadvantaged for employment, the strategies recommended here admittedly will be difficult to put into effect. There are, however, enough examples of successful endeavors to encourage the thought that it is possible. The employment of the strategies described here do result in successes. Many of these can be found among ongoing regular school programs; many others can be found among various programs conducted under recent manpower and related legislation. Two recent successful programs can be cited; they offer concrete illustrations of what can happen when these strategies are brought into play.

The New Haven Pre-Technical Program

A glance at the structure of American education today makes it difficult, if not impossible, to see how immediate progress can be made in the problem under discussion without the utilization and cooperation of the urban elementary and secondary school system. Our first example is therefore drawn from the recent experience in mounting a Pre-Technical Program in the New Haven public schools, with the cooperation of neighboring Quinnipiac College and the Yale-New Haven Medical Center, which received the Gustav-Ohaus Award for "innovative thinking in science curriculum" at the National Science Teachers Association convention in 1969. Authorized in the 1964-65 academic year, this program has to date resulted in lab technician, basic electronics, and animal technician courses in each of the three high schools in the city, where about 25 per cent of the city's total population is nonwhite and where about 50 per cent of public school enrollment is nonwhite.

As is indicated in our first specific strategy, innovative and responsive programs require adequate financial support. The New Haven Board of Education approved the Pre-Technical Program, *provided* that outside funds could be obtained for implementing it. Initially, Ford Foundation funds permitted a pilot program, after which additional monies were forthcoming from state and federal sources as well. In commenting on this aspect of program development, its director says: "The need for large expenditures in this kind of program points out clearly that 'skill or career' education is a very costly venture. Certainly it is more costly than the purely 'academic program' most public schools follow. Traditionalists in secondary school education, and in particular in urban education at this level, in my opinion have not accepted the fundamental idea that 'skill or career educators' is very expensive requiring many more resources than are necessary in the traditional secondary school academic program."

By the same token, program development requires time (it took three years to launch this program) and the cooperative efforts of a myriad of people and institutions, including classroom teachers, administrative school personnel, experts in the substantive areas being scheduled to be taught, community agencies at the local, state and federal levels. In the light of the comments made in this paper on both the money and cooperative personnel needed, as well as on the need for up-to-date equipment, it is interesting to note that all three programs are conducted in conventional classrooms. The basic electronics sequence is taught in classrooms not specifically designed for science instruction—but electronic benches have been constructed by a local company. Similarly, the animal technician course is taught in a regular classroom modified to meet water and caging requirements.

In the matter of access to programs, students are selected from those who are not following a college preparatory course and who are having academic as well as disciplinary problems. Typically, they are students receiving no better than D or F grades, with little or no interest in pursuing their education "not because of lack of ability, but for reasons related to their socio-economic background." To quote the director of the program again: "It is significant to emphasize that while the majority of students selected for these courses are not performing well academically—and frequently have disciplinary problems— these students are *not* 'dopes.' They generally have considerable energy and ingenuity, especially when directed at frustrating the 'system.' The challenge for the public schools is to develop programs which 'harness' this energy and ingenuity and directs it to tasks viewed as purposeful by these students."

One of the significant by-products of this program is a general (but by no means universal) increase in interest in academic subjects, including voluntary tutoring after school and an improvement in over-all attendance. During the past academic year, enrollments were 60 per cent nonwhite in the laboratory technician course, 52 per cent nonwhite in basic electronics, and 46 per cent nonwhite in the animal technician sequence.

The description of the New Haven program talks of a kind of teaching technique and describes it as "genuine individual work guided by patient and competent teachers." When the author asked why teachers were attracted to this program, the answer given by those in charge seemed to describe the magnet of innovative ideas and potentialities. The actual experience in recruiting teachers is instructive.

In the case of laboratory technician, the three New Haven hospitals insisted that their support was predicated on the use of certified medical technologists as teachers, holding that only those practicing personnel could impart to students the kind of attitudes and levels of responsibilities incumbent upon all who operate in a clinical laboratory. This has meant a considerable recruitment problem, as well as obviating state certification rules, and it has also required teacher training programs conducted during the summer months by the staff.

Difficulties were compounded in the recruitment of teachers for the basic electronics courses because of the relatively high pay of practitioners in this field. Faculty have been added from teachers who had developed an "outside" interest in electronics, and special summer training has been provided for teachers at a school of electronics in the city.

Still another dimension was found in the recruitment of personnel for the animal technician curriculum who turned out to be "highly motivated by 'living things'—these teachers had no special skill in animal technology but were extremely enthusiastic about this field." The teachers were trained for this course by a faculty member in the Yale School of Medicine.

One of the more significant results of these programs to date is the very large proportion of students who have decided to go on after high school in pursuit of additional education in their fields. For example, approximately 80 per cent of those completing the basic electronics program are involved in some post high school training in that field and a similar proportion of those completing the laboratory technician program are doing the same in clinical technology.

The success in involving so many of these youth in programs of this sort has led to the development and design of a High School-College Allied Health Careers Program, a joint cooperative effort between the New Haven public school system and neighboring Quinnipiac College, a private institution with a strong sequence in this field. It is a program which features just about every strategy discussed in this paper, involving among other things:

A tandem development of curricula at the high school and college levels, with deliberate counseling in health careers beginning at the seventh grade.

Flexibility in curriculum to permit "changing occupational outcomes with the least amount of sabotage of the individual's past education and experience."

Emphasis on disadvantaged high school students who are not succeeding in academic work.

Developing teacher training for needed faculty.

Integration of facilities of neighboring hospital institutions.

Ability to enter employment on a full-time basis after completion of the high school phase as well as to enter college level work.

As we have noted, there are a wide variety of successful programs dealing with a wide variety of special groups including youthful offenders and armed forces rejectees under manpower legislation. We have highlighted the example of the New Haven program because, like some others, it is attempting to zero in on the problem while the people involved are still in school and presumably are still amenable to preventative rather than remedial action. This is in no way to denigrate the importance of the latter; the chances are the two will always be necessary— from the point of view of the human beings involved as well as the costs. However, the first warrants at least some element of urgency.

The Skill Achievement Institute

As indicated elsewhere in this paper, many of the urban disadvantaged end up in employment at the lowest levels of skill and pay. Their spells of unemployment and their poverty level earnings have serious consequences for their families, which include many of the very urban disadvantaged young people with whom we are concerned. For example, in about one-half of all families living in poverty in the United States, the head of the family is employed, and among these a very large proportion are actually year-round workers. Considerable emphasis has therefore been given to programs of upgrading these people, as the MA-5 system referred to in the previous section is attempting to stimulate.

Because it is operating in this area and because it has had some considerable success in its beginning ventures, we will use as a second case illustration the so-called "high intensity training" efforts of the Skill Achievement Institute, a nonprofit organization funded by the Manpower Administration of the U.S. Department of Labor[11] which manages in-plant training and upgrading projects for underemployed, low-wage workers. This focuses on "black, Spanish-speaking and other workers who have been precluded from moving up into higher paying, more prestigious and influential jobs in both the private and public sectors." The Institute plans the over-all design of the training program and also provides its technical supervision, the in-service training for the plant staff so that it not only leaves behind a newly trained and better utilized and higher paid group of workers but also, it is hoped, some changed attitudes on the part of first-line supervision and a corps of people who can carry no future training programs for plant employees.

What the Institute has found is what exists in substantial numbers in plants throughout the United States; i.e., the existence side by side of large numbers of well-paying jobs going unfilled and a group of unskilled workers poorly paid and considered *a priori* as unqualified to fill them. Access to training for the better jobs within a plant is hampered by many factors; this includes the sheer lack of know-how on how to upgrade attitudes of supervisory and management personnel about the unskilled worker. The Institute's programs are designed to bridge this gap by launching new efforts by employers to re-examine and to make more effective use of their low-skill workers.

One of the basic assumptions involved here, of course, is that the private sector employer is the best agent for change in this field. He has these employees now; he can use their talents if they are upgraded, and he can give trainees higher wages if they are successful. He can gain increased output, reduce waste, and increase the stability of his labor force if the program is success-ful. He also gains a trainer for future programs if he decides to continue. His job structures are examined and often are redone to produce a better organization as well as new promotion opportunities for the underemployed worker.

Upgrading programs are of relatively short duration. The "high intensity programs" used have had considerable success in training workers for higher echelon jobs in good part because they are focused entirely on specific skill achievement with quickly achievable rewards. These programs, however, also take into consideration the person's home as well as work environment, and special efforts are made to motivate low-skill workers to seek added responsibility and raise their level of aspiration. (They get a change in job title and an 8 per cent to 10 per cent increase in wages upon the completion of training.) For example, every upgrading program includes not only the training on work skills required by the target job but also a general orientation on company objectives and human relations training (working with peers and supervisors). "Self develop-ment" is also included—where to go for legal, medical, housing, and related assistance; money management; continuing educa-tion in English language proficiency. The analogies with some of our strategies described above are obvious.

The Institute has stated: "We have found that inclusion of these supplemental objectives helps the program more effectively obtain and maintain the worker's interest, facilitates his learning and retention of technical matter, increases his ambition and desire to learn, and helps make him a more cooperative, goal-oriented employee."

This second case study not only illustrates the potentialities of the continuous system of vocational education and training opportunity described earlier in this paper—in this instance, it extends into the very workplace—but also demonstrates how the private sector can be responsive, in a "businesslike" manner, to its special management and manpower needs.

This emphasizes a final point: We are not going to make a relatively quick and lasting impact on the problem of the vocational education of the urban poor without this kind of engagement by the private sector.

4. Education and Urban Youth

Howard A. Matthews

The fact that there are a multitude of "manpower" programs is evidence that as a nation we have not yet developed a single "manpower policy." At best "manpower" planners find themselves in agreement on only about three things.

First, manpower has something to do with the development of human resources—the development within each individual of the maximum of which he is capable. Second, manpower has something to do with creating employment and other opportunities for each person to nurture his potential; and, third, manpower has something to do with matching these two.

Once having agreed that these three ingredients must pervade all manpower policy, every manpower advocate has different means or methods of bringing the three ingredients into focus.

Some students of the report of the Kerner Commission and several others who have looked at delivery systems for manpower programs suggest that we may have placed far too much emphasis on the "job" as the primary socializing and moralizing influence available to man. The primary emphasis on manpower continues to be almost exclusively "entry-job" oriented.

Among other things, this paper explores briefly the relative role of work (a paycheck) and of industry in the development of human-value systems and suggests that perhaps both really may have been oversold—particularly as far as youths in their formative years are concerned.

In any event, spokesmen for the minorities increasingly suggest that the current emphasis on getting every unemployed person into an entry-job with "meaningful pay" may have the practical effect of insuring that the disadvantaged—the victimized resident of the ghetto who is at the poverty level of income —will continue under current policies to be doing the nation's hard and dirty work, while the man and woman (and their children) who are a cut above the poverty level will be guaranteed a program of educational assistance from the first grade through the Ph.D. The net result, it is asserted by some (the author included), will be an increase in the social and economic distance between the disadvantaged and others in our society rather than a narrowing of it.

This paper explores some of the implications which should be apparent to everyone currently making manpower pronouncements and advocating programs to solve manpower problems. It concludes with some recommendations for the consideration of policy makers, adapted from an article[1] by the author.

Developing Human Resources

The deliberations in recent sessions of the Congress, pronouncements from the White House, and announcements of manpower planning groups suggest that private industry will play an increasingly more active role in training the nation's manpower resources, particularly the disadvantaged. This would be a new role, because historically industry has not been a major training ground for either entry-level employment or for those who are out of school or out of work. Indeed, it has been only within the past year or so that industry's role as a formal trainer of those least prepared for work has been seriously discussed.

If the problems of the disadvantaged are to be solved, the focus of manpower development programs must be directed away from the function of the job itself to the development of unused human resources, particularly those of the disadvantaged. That is, the emphasis must be put on developing the potential of every single individual in our society who needs— and wants—it. Lack of a good job, which is a labor market statistic, is only one of the problems of the disadvantaged.

Ours should be a society in which every individual has the opportunity to achieve his full capabilities. And if this thesis is accepted, it follows that we must also make certain other assumptions and take certain courses of action. For example, we must do whatever is necessary to develop some measures or some means that will help the disadvantaged determine, with reasonable accuracy, his individual capabilities and limitations. More importantly, we must be able somehow to persuade every such individual to turn his "needs" into "wants," to recognize when something is an opportunity to satisfy his "wants"; we must then motivate him to do something about matching one with the other.

Bureaucrats constantly pontificate about what the disadvantaged "need." If the disadvantaged (or anyone for that matter) doesn't know that he needs, what we think he needs— and know it to the point that he *wants* what he needs—nothing productive is likely to happen.

Every era has its myths, and some of the myths of this one are that through mystiques called "standardized" tests, computers, job banks, or some Aldous Huxley test-tube approach, people and opportunities can be matched. It can be seriously questioned whether such measures exist as yet. Experience shows clearly that paper and pencil and other structured tests, particularly those now used by the schools and industry are used to screen people out, not in. Some of the structured tests in use are reasonably accurate for measuring human behavior for the purpose of predicting it; but as instruments for changing human behavior they are pitifully poor, woefully inadequate, and culturally biased.

There is a tendency to oversimplify the problems inherent in developing the potential of human personality. The events that affect people and condition learning and attitudinal patterns, and the myriad phenomena that influence what people do (or don't do) are assumed to have simple cause and effect relationships. "Job-oriented" programs for ghetto residents presume a simple cause and effect sequence: Get a person on a payroll and all his problems will be solved.

Paradoxically, the knowledge explosion of today and the complexities of its application to specific situations work to destroy rather than to create rational cause and effect sequences and relationships. They confuse and make more uncertain possible alternatives to most decisions. With more alternatives to consider and with more uncontrollable and unidentifiable variables, simple cause and effect sequences and relationships are not only obscure but are also impossible to isolate. Events tend increasingly to happen all at once and rather in casual, circular, and probabilistic ways. It has even been suggested by some social scientists that we may be approaching—without really knowing it—the end of rational vision in decision making.[2]

Increasingly, the forces that control the activities of people in general—particularly ghetto residents—and the services they need or want are being truncated by the very profusion of local agencies of the government. Take, for example, a single community near Chicago. It has two counties, three townships, a village, four school districts, a sanitary district, a mosquito abatement district, and a tuberculosis sanitarium district. All of these units have differing boundaries. Each of these entities was created by a distinct law or set of laws passed by the state legislature, and few of them, if any, are controlled or supervised by a centralized or coordinating agency of government. Each is managed by a single autonomous administrative board, council, or commission whose rules and regulations (administrative laws) have the force and effect of statute law. Under such "administrative laws," each board or its administrator can invoke sanctions that are equally as valid and binding on minorities and others as the statute laws passed by state legislatures or by the Congress or as the decisions of the U.S. Supreme Court.

Within the over-all Standard Metropolitan Statistical Area (SMSA)[3] of Chicago, in which the community described above lies, there were, at last report, six counties, 246 municipalities, 114 township governments, 340 school districts, and 354 special districts. This inter-governmental complex involves over six million people.[4]

These are the units of government which have the personal contact with people needing services. Each unit was created through the legislative process in response to the needs of people who have demanded, or required, certain specific services.

A recent census analysis shows that more than a half-million elected public officials preside over such local units of government throughout the country. Over half of these units serve fewer than a thousand persons.[5] The National Commission on Urban Problems in its report to the Congress and to the President on December 12, 1968, found that most of these local governmental units—particularly those related to large urban areas—were extremely small, geographically. Among other things, the report says that about one-half of the municipalities in the average SMSA have less than a single square mile of land area. Probably 60 per cent are smaller than two square miles, and four-fifths have a land area less than four square miles. Fewer than 200 SMSA municipalities in the United States include as much as twenty-five square miles of land. The average SMSA central city has more than four overlaying local governments![6]

On the average, there are about ninety units of government

per SMSA, and the average resident of any metropolitan area is served by at least four separate local governments, i.e., county, municipality or township; one or more school districts, plus from one to perhaps a dozen separate special districts concerned with rats, sewers, mosquitoes, dogs, pollution of some sort or another, zoning regulations, etc. In addition to having differing population boundaries, and purpose, local units seldom follow the same procedures and practices in exercising their rule-making powers.

The racial, ethnic, religious, or other characteristics which identify minority groups also tend to complicate the problem by creating the geographical dispersion of minority groups known as de facto segregation. A different minority group mix is found as one moves across local jurisdiction boundaries.

Imagine the confusion that exists when the inner-city ghetto resident attempts to struggle through this administrative agency labyrinth. Suppose that a member or leader of a local minority group wanted to question a rise in his property taxes in terms of the programs of his school or those he thinks are somehow related to the school. With property taxes levied upon him by three to six separate local taxing units, to which should his protest go?

Congress and various associations of state and local officials are now searching for *the* coordinating mechanism. Meanwhile, until such a mechanism can be found to minimize the uncoordinated operation and overlapping of local governmental agencies, it is essential to achieve some consistency in the practices followed by these entities in performing the public's business and providing human services. (It should be recognized that even the creation of some federal system may *not* induce states to coordinate services or make it attractive for them to bring about coordination at the local level.)

Whatever the institutional considerations involved here, it should be emphasized that merely getting a person on a payroll may actually complicate his problems—rather than ushering in the millennium for him—because a new pattern of life emerges which is foreign to him. Let us assume that a single agency, office, or organization is given the responsibility for assuring that each person in our society is guaranteed at least one opportunity to achieve his maximum potential (which he more than often does not recognize). Let us also make certain that the changes take place that are necessary in his social and working environment to guarantee that he has this chance to achieve this potential. Wouldn't it also follow that such an agency would also have to be given a much greater latitude in manipulating people than is now granted? What agency do we give it to? How are the rights of the individual as a citizen safeguarded? Who would be willing to assign this much authority to a federal, state, county, or city unit of government or to some combination thereof?

Would the responsibility of matching people with opportunities be vested in the public or in the private sector? Are private, profit-making industries best able to assume this responsibility? This is a question that should be answered in the context of the interest and rights of the individuals and the history of the labor movement.

Let it be assumed for purposes of debate that private industry *is* the place to fix the responsibility. If it is, then it must be remembered that several considerations must permeate all industry planning. First, any company, including the industrial giant, must be operated in such a way to guarantee a profit; and this must be taken into account in everything that is done— pious words and moral pronouncements to the contrary notwithstanding.

As a matter of practical fact, while this does not mean that everything that a given industry does at any single moment in time must render profit, it *does* mean that the enterprise as a whole over any specified period of time must show a profit. Training must obviously be considered in this light. Second, it must be remembered that because industry, including only those selling education in the marketplace, has to assume that it is going to be in business for as long into the future as anyone can see, it simply cannot make long-range decisions by pragmatically looking at the money that can be made next week or six months from now on a federal Job Opportunities in the Business Sector (JOBS) contract. If programs for the ghetto disadvantaged are to be inexpensive, and if they are to be woven into the fabric of industry on a long-range basis, industrial planners must also consider such programs in the light of the constraints caused by union contracts, competition, obsolescence of the skills of people, equipment, processes, tax laws, and many other forces.

It is also important to recognize that manpower predictions made today based on reasonable projections of technological advancements can be rendered obsolete almost overnight by unanticipated change and innovation.[7] Many individual industries admit that they find it impossible to project total or even partial training needs or production schedules over any appreciable period of time. Very few companies can predict with any degree of accuracy even five years from now the types of hardware they will have in the marketplace, what major products they will sell or buy, and what specific types of skills they will need to do so.

Current manpower studies suggest that perhaps the best analysis of industrial manpower needs for the years ahead can only be stated in very broad and vague occupational categories rather than in terms of specific job requirements, e.g., agricultural, managerial, technical, as opposed to machinists, keypunch operators, etc. This state of the arts also suggests that perhaps the most effective pre-employment training of ghetto and other youngsters for jobs of the future may be that which is very broadly based, enabling an individual to function in a number of jobs throughout his work life, many of which may actually be unrelated as to content or skill requirements.[8] Skill training narrowly conceived simply cannot accomplish this, although some types of it, in the author's view, have much more transfer value than educators have recognized in the past.

All too often, unfortunately, the sponsors and advocates of federal programs, as well as some members of the Congress, have wanted to show dramatic results in reducing unemployment or underemployment in terms of a few weeks or months through one crash program or another. There is no question that we can speed up the educational planning process as well as the schedules for teaching and reduce the time traditionally taken in training for a specific job, as the Manpower Development and Training Act (MDTA) of 1962 has demonstrated. However, in spite of all the dramatic developments in the technology and hardware for learning, and no matter how many hours of training are scheduled per week, the human eye can still only see certain frequencies between infra-red and ultraviolet, and the human ear can only acknowledge certain types of vibrations. Perhaps in more ways than are generally acknowledged, the theoretical limit in the application of certain technologies to learning have been reached, and insistence on performance beyond these natural barriers may only be frustrating to both teacher and student.

Jerome Wiesner has suggested that it takes at least twenty years between the discovery of a new scientific principle and its forceful impact on industry, as in the case of the transistor. Our computers are based on discoveries in physics and fundamental science that go back thirty, forty, or even fifty years.[9] Implementing new ideas in industry training or in public education is analogous to the difficulties encountered by Farnsworth in developing the basic principles of television. These ideas simply could not be put into effect until he had secured the use of a host of related processes previously patented. Likewise, even within a single corporation as within some school systems, built-in bureaucracies with vested interests impede innovation and progress, and often just cannot be moved by normal forces and processes.

Moreover, there is little evidence to suggest that the production or work processes in private industry are adaptable per se—i.e., as an *integral part of the production process*—to education programs in such a way that they can bring about major benefits to large numbers of disadvantaged persons (including those out of work, particularly those who are underemployed and out of the mainstream of society). There is, in fact, mounting evidence that suggests industry either cannot or will not attempt such programs. A more effective approach to the educational problems of the disadvantaged is offered by cooperative occupational programs, which are emphasized by the Vocational Education Act of 1968. Under these arrangements, which link industry with colleges, universities, schools of all types, and other social agencies, the schools accept full responsibility for all phases of the program. This approach seems more compatible with the aspirations both of the unemployed and of industry as well.

The attempt to place responsibility for encouraging human renewal through educational or training programs raises another theoretical question. Should the impact of any financial inducement or any other approach to human self-renewal be directed to the individual? Or should some other mechanism be utilized to create opportunities and motivate people, to bring people and opportunities together? Since the method through which funds are dispersed usually has a direct effect upon the motivation of the individual, a good deal hangs on the answer to this question.

Tax incentives to industry[10] have been suggested as an approach to the problem. Yet how can they be used to provide motivation for the man hustling a buck on the corner? He is both unaffected and uninterested. Even more important, how do you protect him against exploitation by industry? And, how do you avoid paying industry for doing what it is already doing?

Even a superficial analysis of current manpower data suggests that there is a very high and positive correlation between the amount of formal training a person has and his attachment to the labor force.[11] Does this suggest that for all practical purposes, attachment to the working world is really governed in the final analysis more by the "mental ingredient"—the education and training, attitudes, aspirations, and fears—than by the mechanical or manipulative application of this ingredient to performance tasks and jobs? Does this also suggest that perhaps the most effective way to develop a lasting attachment to the labor force for the unemployed and underemployed is to broaden their formal conceptual training, while at the same time raising their aspirations and hope for long-range success?

The Role of Work

There is great need for a careful and cautious reappraisal of the role of "work" in the human value-system by those doing manpower planning and setting manpower policy.

Until about a decade ago, we were a production-oriented society. The majority of our labor force was engaged in producing goods—tangible articles or products with which it was relatively easy for each person to identify in terms of his own individual physical and mental efforts and from which he gained a measure of self-respect and fulfillment. In substance, there was a reasonably simple cause and effect relationship between work and real and psychic reward. For most people a job was both a socializing and moralizing influence. The "right" thing to do was to get and hold a job. There was even some lingering vestige of economic usefulness for our young while they were still young.

Things have changed. We are a service and sales oriented society, which has more people selling goods and services than it has producing goods, running the farms, and building houses and factories. At the same time, there has also been a narrowing overspecialization of tasks, whether these are employed in producing goods, sales, or services. People fail to find a significant identification with something in which they can take personal pride of accomplishment and receive fulfillment. Even in production or "goods" oriented tasks, man is increasingly a machine baby-sitter, who is conditioned to respond in terms of what to do when the red light appears on the panel and not really in terms of what caused the light to go on in the first place, or how to keep it from happening again.[12] He knows only his job is going well if nothing happens. When it does, someone else fixes it.

The problem is further compounded when we consider that the production or goods-based aspect of work is directly related to the Protestant-Puritan ethic of work accented by the industrial revolution. The work-reward ethic in our value system says that from his labors man is entitled to leisure and to his stake in the hereafter. He works first, then gets a paycheck and earns vacation time; from work comes the good life.

Like it or not, this ethic or value system of work in terms of holding down a payroll job has all but vanished. Few people work now because it is the decent moral thing to do. Indeed, the point has now been reached where this country may be the only so-called civilized nation in the entire history of Western civilization that has absolutely no economic use for our young while they are young—unless giving a kid two bits for carrying out the garbage or $1.65 an hour for picking up paper in the Neighborhood Youth Corps, or exploiting him over television is regarded as economic use.

The simple fact is that the job and the function of being on a payroll are no longer a socializing or moralizing influence for lots of people. Many disadvantaged people have told me that they accepted training for a specific, predetermined job— not because they think the job held out to them is going to really improve their life significantly, but because they have to work to get a steady flow of money.

The evidence is abundantly clear that many people at all social strata in our society can and do derive almost all of their self-renewal, personal satisfactions, and fulfillments from body gratifications and activities other than those associated with what gives them a paycheck. As evidence, consider only such things as the "happenings" on the ghetto streets for both the fortunate and the less fortunate and on the campuses, or the beaches of California and Ocean City for the more affluent. Or, in a positive vein, the Peace Corps and VISTA Volunteers. In my judgment, it is both unjust and dangerous to convince anyone—through any means, including such euphemisms as "employability skills" training—that his major satisfactions and self-renewals will come when he is on a job, and then be unable, as we are more often than not, to help him get that type of a job. The same thing is true about training programs.

Bernard J. Wohl, Executive Director of the South Side Settlement in Columbus, Ohio, told the Congress that:

> We are critical of those programs which have attempted to train and hire the poor because those who were fortunate enough to be accepted into these programs have in essence been "bought off" and are no longer in the struggle to guarantee for all of their fellow citizens the jobs that they need so desperately. It has created divisiveness and despair instead of concern and participation. Our approach has been to deal with employment as we would deal with any other problem, in a wholistic manner. We continue to struggle with the youth and adults of our community to seek programs and services that are inclusive rather than exclusive in nature. And if we are really serious about jobs for all, let us not talk and develop "make work employment" or places "to keep kids off the street" as a type of "aging vat" which helps them serve time and helps them get older and better adjusted to their poverty. Let us develop programs that inject a value system into our approach where challenge and open and honest questioning can take place where our goals are directed towards social justice rather than social control . . . [13]

As a matter of fact, the real world that is creating the value systems of today's youngsters in their formative years tells them loud and clear that leisure isn't the reward for hard work. Our credit-card culture tells them to travel, or otherwise enjoy, first and pay later—which reverses the cause and effect work-reward sequence and says that, in reality, work may at best be psychologically a punishment for having enjoyed or taken the leisure first. Or, of course, it could mean that more and more people of all ages are coming to believe that there is no longer a need or excuse to work—hold a job that gives them a paycheck just in order to comfortably enjoy life, take leisure, or otherwise find self-expression, usefulness, and fulfillment.[14]

Ross Stagner, Chairman of the Department of Psychology at Wayne State University agrees. He recently said that:

> I would like to say, incidentally, that we hold up this notion of jobs as one of the important components of this policy (manpower policy). Every man—and I suppose, according to some people at least, every woman—ought to have a job and our social policy should be directed toward providing these jobs and, I suppose, insisting that people take a job even if they don't want to. I don't think this is quite necessary. . . . However, I think that most people probably would concede, on the whole, that there is no justification for the notion that a man has to have a job. What he requires is a position in which he can respect himself and be respected by other people. . . . What I am saying is that we need to approach this problem in terms of human motives. The motives involved here are the desire for self-respect and the desire for the respect of other people. We can achieve that in many ways other than through productive employment . . . [15]

Many suggest that we ought to be able to assume that leisure or non-working enjoyment should have meaning in addition to that associated with recreation and hobbies.[16] But it is hard to see how the state of mind required for this is going to be developed in young people who go through an educational system stressing efficiency, and whose parents and teachers are for the most part products of both this educational system and of the Protestant-Puritan ethic with its work-reward sequence. Tranquillity, contemplation, loafing, and the cultivation of self suggest a different kind of home, parents, school, and different types of teachers than now exist. Just how real or serious the social consequences are in these observations remains to be seen. It seems obvious, however, that we have not studied the problem and we have not tried to lay out its implications in a sufficiently elaborate social and educational context to give us any clues to the future.[17]

Some indicators seem to exist, however. Helen M. Harris, Executive Director of the United Neighborhood Houses of New York, tells[18] of a teacher in a low-income New York neighborhood who asked her sixth-grade pupils one day what kinds of jobs their fathers had. When they could not reply, she asked more questions, only to discover that the word "work" as associated with a job in the tradition of the Protestant-Puritan ethic was not in their vocabularies in relation to earning a living. Most of them had no fathers at home; they were either dead or had deserted. The majority of the families were on welfare, and had been for as long as these children could remember. They had absolutely no idea about the traditional role of *work* or of a *job* in our society, or of the different kinds of jobs people have, or can have, which most children learn from the experience of the breadwinner and other workers in the usual middle-class family.[19] There are a multitude of implications in the situation described by Mrs. Harris.

For example, in the United States there are nearly five million boys under the age of eighteen (and six million girls) who live in fatherless homes—who have no opportunity to learn about the world of work from a male breadwinner. In fact, over a million and a half such boys live in homes where neither natural parent is present. As the public schools are increasingly unable to compete in the marketplace for male teachers—particularly for the lower elementary grades—many of these boys will not have had an opportunity to develop a wholesome adult "male image" before they drop out of school and will live all of their formative years in a female-dominated environment. Their male image will consist chiefly of the garbage collector, the cop on the corner, a "pusher," the local delicatessen operator, or a school principal whom they usually see on a personal basis only when they get into trouble. What are the social consequences and have we really studied or prepared for them?

In the current blind rush of government to industry, and in many instances to service-oriented industries, how well-prepared psychologically will these boys be to be trained for and accept jobs where the supervisors have traditionally been women, and where most of the other employees are also women? I know of instances where boys trained in federal programs have refused jobs because they would be supervised by women.

To compound the same problem, an eminent psychiatrist has suggested that as tomorrow's society becomes more and more service oriented, in order to be employed many men will have to take jobs which traditionally in our society have been women's roles, i.e., person-to-person helping roles. What then happens to this "male" image in the value system of the young and to the conduct normally expected of men? What happens to the relation between the sexes as the hard won pattern of women competing with men for "male" jobs is reversed, and men begin to compete with women for "female" jobs, or has the so-called male image already vanished from our value system?[20]

Another question we need to consider along these lines is the future of the unskilled women now employed in the work force. At present about one-third of our work force are women, about 80 per cent of whom are no more than semiskilled. Many of them do the clerical and routine service jobs, which automation will continue to replace as its application is accelerated by the increasing number as well as the increasing size of organizations and institutions responding to both the population and technological explosions.

Now about 60 per cent of the $9,000 to $15,000 a year incomes of this country are in families where both husband and wife work. If it happens that there is less employment for unskilled women it would follow—wouldn't it—that there will be less family income and therefore less consumption, less production, and probably fewer over-all employment opportunities. And there is the problem of psychic income. Many women work for reasons other than to earn money. What will provide this psychic income?[21]

Perhaps jobs could be created, particularly in the human services area, which retrained women could fill and which, because of the interpersonal nature of the task are not likely to be automated. As it now stands, however, and the manpower and poverty program clearly demonstrates this, we are neither seriously creating these jobs, nor are we making the extensive effort needed to motivate women (or men, for that matter) to be retrained or upgraded for new jobs while they are employed and long before their current job runs out.

This problem undoubtedly will become more serious, particularly for women who are heads of households, before techniques for job-producing, motivating, recruiting, and training are sufficiently developed to cope with it.[22] Furthermore, another pretty sure bet is that, if we *do* develop such techniques, tomorrow's society will become tremendously different from today's because the roles of so many women will be so different from what they always have been.

The Kerner Commission report as well as the studies of the Joint Economic Committee of the Senate and the House also suggest that our manpower policies and practices have over emphasized the idea that all the disadvantaged wants or needs is a job.[23] Those who have studied the effects of jobs on people (Peter Drucker, for example) have said that probably the worst thing that can be done for any individual, including the disadvantaged of all types, is to train them so well for their first job that all too often they are locked in by archaic union-management bargaining contracts, industry traditions, and similar situations. Historically, such institutionalized arrangements treated promotion and upward mobility more as functions of seniority than of educational competence, and their persistence shows a failure to recognize that the impact of technology demands a better educated worker at all levels.[24]

The disadvantaged tell me that such jobs can be had, and most who get jobs do so through friends or on their own, even after MDTA programs. They also tell me that money can be had. There is, in fact, a significant economy even in the ghetto, however illegal it might be—numbers, prostitution, pushing, and other forms of "hustle." Dollars do turn over.

What they really seek and have a right to aspire to are the same middle and upper class status symbols we all seek. They want the skills and abilities which will allow them the same cafeteria selection of status jobs we hold. They don't want someone putting them through a counseling and testing mystique and then telling them what they "need," putting a "meat stamp" on them as "Grade A" for a certain manpower program, and sending them somewhere to acquire what someone else had decided is their "bag."

They reject strenuously a single desk telling them what job is "best" for them. The disadvantaged also tell me that a certificate from industry X saying that Joe Grow can assemble wires on that particular industry's hardware isn't what they want in the long haul, because it just won't buy them much, if anything, with an industry competitor, and it is not nearly as saleable in the general job marketplace as a certificate of high school equivalency or a school or college diploma. They, too, prefer both the status and the job mobility the latter gives them.

Intuitively, the disadvantaged ghetto resident knows that

the job hierarchy setup that Marcia Freedman describes in her study of two large utilities is the real scene.[25] Dr. Freedman found that variance in individual promotions could be largely explained by employees' length of service, whether these promotions were meaningful (title changes reflecting skill differences and more pay) or were nominal routine promotions requiring relatively little screening. While specific courses were sometimes significant, years of formal education achievement accounted for little in meaningful variance in *promotion practices*. Dr. Freedman also found that most of the substantive promotions actually took place in the early years of service, thereby serving to "lock" employees both into firms for which they worked and into specific jobs.[26] Finding himself in this predicament, the disadvantaged person tends to "blow the scene" because hope for the future for better status jobs becomes little more than a daydream.

Vocational educators and manpower planners should learn from these findings the importance of studying through follow-up research the organizational career experiences of their students and building the lessons of such research into the vocational curriculum. It is important to note that in Freedman's study she found that providing educational credentials helped more than anything else get a person a job in the work establishment. What then became important for young people was an ability to negotiate or manipulate organizational systems and patterns.

This also suggests that organizational success really goes to those who "hang in" there, in turn making the question of initial job choice *at higher than entry level* all the more significant. That this choice process is ragged has already been demonstrated by researchers whose data show that job-seeking is largely an accidental process.[27]

In the Freedman study, it was also found that in four large employer organizations in the New York City area, job titles were more often than not only nominally different. Skill differences did not, in fact, actually constitute a very differentiated job hierarchy. Organizational know-how counted most, and this know-how is learned only in organizations, not in school. Because of seniority and organizational rigidity, two-year trained technicians became discouraged because they more often than not had to start low in the title hierarchy. Having done this, they came to realize very soon that they would have been better off had they been guided and helped into engineering programs rather than two-year technical programs, because a *degree* would have qualified them for a higher level entry job and a better start in the "system."

There is little evidence that significant long-range manpower planning is taking place to change the types of manpower-educational problems discussed above as private industry is courted and wooed by government to train the disadvantaged and do the things they always should have done.

Also in need of more examination is what can the schools—better, what should the schools—be doing to help bring about long-range solutions to these types of problems, the schools being the only agency that has all of the youngsters at some time during their formative years.

As industry that contemplates undertaking a partnership with government, or the role of employer or trainer of the disadvantaged, we should re-examine some of its own training program philosophies, such as the idea that all people somehow profit from both job experience and training. This may have been true once, but no longer.

Because of the rapidity of technological change and the increased importance of mental skills at the expense of manual strength and dexterity and years of experience, many industries have found that they now need, and are likely to go on needing, a much higher caliber of work and supervision than they have in the past. For this reason, and for many others, there has been little time and money spent or expertise developed by industry in training employees of low caliber. While it may be true that every person can derive some residual benefit from training, the effort and costs involved in keeping an entire work force constantly involved in some type of training undoubtedly would exceed the cost-benefit ratio of the economic survival—unless, of course, government increasingly picks up the tab.

Another basic assumption regarding industry training in need of serious re-examination is that all training in industry is good—that training by industry can (by itself) cure most of the problems of unemployment and underemployment.[28] This assumption is, of course, related to another of the prevailing myths, namely, that a job—being put on the payroll—can solve most of the problems of the disadvantaged and cure most of their ills. Both the assumption and the myth derive from the premise that most problems are the result of the lack of job experience, which in turn is caused mostly by inadequate formal job preparation. They also derive in part from the historical ethic of "work" previously discussed.

There simply are many situations that training or job experience cannot remedy. They cannot counteract unwise promotions, outdated seniority policies, or ineffective methods, nor can either training or job experience replace intelligent supervision, favorable environmental conditions, individual unwillingness to accept responsibility, and the like. Furthermore, when industry conducted training is seen as a panacea, executives and supervisory personnel alike easily cover up their own inadequacies by assigning all of their production or management problems to deficiencies in their subordinates' training. They didn't provide the "right" training.

It must be remembered that in industry, "right" can mean anything from "there's no proof to the contrary" to "we have to cover up this blunder for the sake of the company." Blind faith that on-the-job training is the "right" thing to do for the disadvantaged ghetto resident often results in establishing training divisions in industry vested only with the authority for developing people at the lower levels of the organizations. This, in turn, often leads line supervisors to believe that training is no longer part of their responsibility. Such abdication, wherever it happens, is really very much like trying to delegate the authority for handling all human problems to the personnel department—something that would be regarded as preposterous by the managers and personnel men alike.[29] And it is akin to trying to legislate leadership, morality, and brotherly love.

There is a tendency among those promoting so-called industry on-the-job training to ignore the simple truth that today there are at least two types of industry training. First, there is that training which industry has traditionally done for itself—to satisfy its own needs for updating its internal labor force—including production, supervision, and management personnel. Some government and Congressional manpower advocates are under the misguided assumption that the disadvantaged hired through JOBS, NAB, or manpower administrators are all being included in this facet of industry training.

The second type of industry training stems from the practical economic fact that there is virtually no risk involved, and often a whole lot more profit, in merchandising crash government-sponsored, cost-plus, paid-for education and training in the marketplace than there is coming up with and selling the proverbial new mouse trap. Consequently, much of the highly touted on-the-job training is not really training at the job site in a production task in the industry that is conducting the government-sponsored program, but rather heavily subsidized, classroom institutional training for the general labor marketplace in competition with public and other private schools and training agencies—and at tremendously higher cost to the taxpayer.

Often the outfit peddling such education and training in the marketplace in competition with the established private and public schools is a separate division within the corporate structure of the company. More often than not it is not even remotely related to the training division of the company, which has historically existed and which trains the company's internal labor force.[30]

Capitalizing on the current poor image of public education in general (which is property-tax starved) and vocational education in particular, some such private industries have engaged in cutthroat practices to get manpower program contracts, rather than joining hands with the schools to improve both financing and image. This type of behavior is hardly befitting the elevated station to which industry has been raised by current manpower policies and pronouncements.

When one looks at the actual course content of some of these so-called industry training programs, he is apt to find that they have few if any concepts or approaches that are new, imaginative or innovative. In far too many instances private industry has merely taken a pair of scissors and a paste jar and put together courses of study previously developed at federal, state, and/or local expense. To these they have added a few management terms such as "feedback and response training mechanism," "instant mental reinforcement," etc. A visit to the classroom usually reveals nothing new, different or innovative—only a more expensive process than doing it through such proven programs as the MDTA Skills Centers.

Summary and Suggestions

Today, the terms "education" and "manpower" are virtually synonymous. When they are not, they should be. Two assumptions must pervade all manpower policy. First, within every job (from the research physicist to the custodian) skills are changing, and in the future there will be increasingly less emphasis on years of experience and more emphasis on education. Second, a radically increasing number of jobs already put a premium on general intellectual alertness, on ability to read well and compute accurately, analyze and solve problems, and work cooperatively with others. These are educational needs of people and of society and not of schools, universities, and institutions. These are our manpower needs. Educational leaders must become concerned with more than only what people do in the traditional teaching-learning classroom situation.

What really should concern us then is education as a whole, recognizing that it has a great many functions and purposes. Education, like electricity, is easier to define in terms of its effects while in motion than in terms of its actual composition.

The educational needs of society will be met only when we develop more and better education opportunities at all levels from the nursery to the university. The following recommendations are intended to bring about this reform.

1.   In order to play something more than a passive role in social change, all schools at all grade levels must organize themselves to be able to respond quickly and effectively to sudden technological changes. They must be able to provide educational experiences which will assist people in making short and long-term adjustments to changing social and economic conditions whenever they happen.

2.   More active and comprehensive educational planning by school officials in all types of school administrative units and by the leadership of the community must be developed and nurtured. School board members and school administrators whom I know are making forces for change (such as automation) positive influences. To do so, they constantly seek the advice of business, labor, universities, agriculture, and other interested groups. They are designing responsive educational systems that will at any point in time provide programs suited to the emerging needs of the community. At the same time, however, one of the most justified criticisms of public schools at all levels is that they fail to anticipate change and take deliberate steps to prepare for it.

3.   Evaluation is just as much a part of planning a new course or program as is the housing of it. Programs must be redirected whenever evaluation suggests that they need to be

changed. Many teachers, particularly those at the post-high school level, not only do not know to what extent they are effective but also do not care. With the crowded classrooms and more seeking admission than can be accommodated, they don't have to care. In addition, tests of their own making, reflecting not what the student knows—or necessarily needs to know—but what the teacher thinks is important, often prevent careful analysis.

4.   Schools are not the only training agencies in society. Labor unions and industry which are involved in apprentice programs and on-the-job training should, like the schools, be asking themselves searching questions: Is it possible, for instance, to accelerate some of these programs and do, say, in three years or less what we are now convinced takes five? Perhaps apprenticeship is as in need of evaluation and updating as traditional school vocational programs.

5.   Educational opportunities must be available to people throughout their lives or the needs of today as well as tomorrow will not be met. Ability to manage change—whether keeping up with developments in professions or retooling for new jobs—requires education experiences to be available when they are needed. Access to education governs the pace at which new knowledge is absorbed and adjustments made to new technologies, and solutions reached to related social, political, and economic problems. The lifelong learning process goes on not only in the classroom, the extension course, and the lecture series, but through individual reading, television, instruction on the assembly line, and even at coffee break. A well-balanced system of continuing public education must provide a comprehensive program of educational opportunity for persons with varying educational attainments in all areas of the state. The high school dropout must be able to find a program which encourages re-entry to school, and the Ph.D. an opportunity to probe more deeply into a special field or to broaden his general background.

Such possibilities require an open-ended educational system with students free to enter, to leave when other experiences seem more fruitful, then to re-enter. In order to assist the disadvantaged, programs must be designed without regard for the traditional conventional administrative (but not educational) conveniences of quarters, semesters, six-week or nine-week terms, Carnegie units, and quarter-hour and semester-hour formulas. Flexible programs must be developed so the students may leave to take a job at any time or stay for advanced school work without regard for the time of day, the school calendar, or the college catalog. Such a system can become a reality only through the coordinated efforts of public schools, community colleges, vocational schools, universities, and employers. The educational process, beginning at the most basic levels, must also impress upon the individual that he has responsibility for continuing self-education and self-renewal to achieve a meaningful adaptation to a constantly changing environment.

6.   There is a special need for broader and deeper opportunities for those adults whose basic education is deficient. Over 25 million members of the present labor force lack high school diplomas. Some eight million have not completed the eighth grade. One-sixth of American youth cannot qualify for military service because they are unable to pass a seventh grade equivalency test. Yet, open-ended opportunities for adult basic education are few, and knowledge of how to overcome the problems of teaching adults is meager.

7.   Retraining programs must be expanded rapidly so that a significant percentage of the local labor force is retrained annually. The training provided thus far by the Manpower Development and Training Act has demonstrated that a significant capacity for training and retraining exists outside the public school framework. It has also uprooted some entrenched ideas about how long it takes for the American worker to develop the skills necessary for an entry-level job, for entering apprenticeship or on-the-job training.

8. There is increasing evidence that perhaps the most effective way to retrain disadvantaged people—whether displaced as a result of automation or underemployed because of social and economic disadvantages—is through cooperative education programs. In such "person-centered" programs, the school develops instruction best suited to the classroom and helps a potential employer develop specific work skills at the job site. The total training responsibility, however, rests with the school.

It has been far too common in our tradition of mass, free education to blame failure on the shortcomings of the student and to neglect innovative techniques which could change institutions to meet students' needs. Reducing economic barriers with income maintenance programs helps those who can respond to well-established techniques of formal education. But it does little for those, either in or out of school, who cannot make effective use of established training patterns. The task must focus, then, on adjusting the system to meet the needs of people who cannot be reached through existing educational methods.

In short, more educational programs of high quality must be made available. But the word "quality" should not be confused with sophistication of course content. "High quality programs" are those with adequate resources, well-trained teachers, suitable buildings, necessary income maintenance and human services, and appropriate curricula and educational methods. These are possible only through partnerships between agencies of the federal, state and local governments, private employers, and trade associations, labor unions, and the rest of the community. The beneficiary of this careful planning and cooperation is the individual in the first instance. In the long run, society as a whole can be expected to benefit.

Notes

Chapter 2. Preparing Youth for Employment (pages 24-51)

1. Rupert N. Evans, "School for Schooling's Sake: The Current Role of the Secondary School in Occupational Preparation," in Princeton Manpower Symposium, *The Transition from School to Work; A Report* (Princeton: Princeton University, Industrial Relations Section, 1968).

2. Garth L. Mangum, *Reorienting Vocational Education* (Ann Arbor: University of Michigan, Institute of Labor and Industrial Relations, 1968), pp. 46-52; reprinted in Sar A. Levitan and Garth L. Mangum, *Federal Training and Work Programs in the Sixties* (Ann Arbor: University of Michigan, Institute of Labor and Industrial Relations, 1969), pp. 149-155; quoting in part from U.S. Advisory Council on Vocational Education, *Vocational Education; The Bridge Between Man and His Work; General Report* (Washington, D.C.; U.S. Government Printing Office, 1968); reprinted in Rupert N. Evans, Garth L. Mangum, and Otto Pragan, *Education for Employment: The Background and Potential of the 1968 Vocational Education Amendments* (Ann Arbor: University of Michigan, Institute of Labor and Industrial Relations, 1969), pp. 63-67.

3. Marvin J. Feldman, *Public Education and Manpower Development* (New York: Ford Foundation, 1967).

4. That is, those not products of the dominant culture.

5. Sar A. Levitan and Garth L. Mangum, *op. cit.*, pp. 141-142.

6. Marvin J. Feldman, *Making Education Relevant* (New York: Ford Foundation, 1966).

7. Sar A. Levitan and Garth L. Mangum, *op. cit.*, pp. 142-147.

8. Sar A. Levitan and Garth L. Mangum, *op. cit.*, pp. 144-145.

9. Garth L. Mangum, "Vocational Education for the Disadvantaged: Lessons from Government Funded Programs," paper presented at the National Workshop on Vocational Education for the Disadvantaged, Atlantic City, New Jersey, March 12-14, 1969 (New York: National Committee on Employment of Youth). See also papers of Marvin J. Feldman, Richard Greenfield, Martin Hamburger, and Jerry C. Olson as relevant to this paper though not to this point.

Chapter 3. Seven Strategies for Success (pages 52-82)

1. Gordon Swanson, "Action in Vocational Education Considered as Social Protest," *Phi Delta Kappan*, Vol. 46, No. 8 (April 1965), pp. 353-354.

2. John Fischer, *The Stupidity Problem and Other Harassments* (New York: Harper & Row, 1964).

3. U.S. Congress. House. Committee on Education and Labor, *Manpower Development and Training Act of 1961; Report to Accompany H.R. 8399* (Washington, D.C.: U.S. Government Printing Office, August 10, 1961), p. 27.

4. Lowell A. Burkett, "Access to a Future," *American Education*, Vol. 5, No. 3 (March 1969), pp. 2-3.

5. Public Law 90-576, approved October 16, 1968.

6. For example, see Dorothea Kahn Jaffe, "High Schoolers Join Co-op Corps," *The Christian Science Monitor* (June 3, 1969), p. 9.

7. National Alliance of Businessmen. *JOBS, Request for Proposal MA-5* (Washington, D.C.: May 1969).

8. See the section, "Operational Insights from E & D Projects," in U.S. President, *Manpower Report of the President* (Washington, D.C.: U.S. Government Printing Office, 1969).

9. U.S. National Advisory Commission on Civil Disorders, *Report* (New York: Bantam Books, 1968), pp. 444-445.

10. J. McGavack, "New Haven's Pre-Technical Program" (New Haven: New Haven Public Schools, January 1969).

11. Materials on these programs are from the Skill Achievement Institute, 179 Community Drive, Great Neck, N.Y. 11021.

Chapter 4. Education and Urban Youth (pages 83-109)

1. Howard A. Matthews, "Tomorrow Is Now," *American Education*, Vol. 3, No. 6 (June 1967), pp. 21-22.

2. Daniel Bell, "The Post-Industrial Society," in Columbia University. Seminar on Technology and Social Change, *Technology and Economic Change*, ed. by Eli Ginzberg (New York: Columbia University Press, 1964), pp. 58-59.

3. A Bureau of the Census term for a socially and economically describable area.

4. Edmund S. Muskie, "The Challenge of Creative Federalism," *Congressional Record* (Washington, D.C.: U.S. Government Printing Office, 1966), Vol. 112, Part 5, p. 6834.

5. Henry S. Reuss, "The State and Local Government Modernization Act of 1969: A Program of Federal Grants to States Which Take Steps To Modernize State and Local Governments," *Congressional Record* (Washington, D.C.: U.S. Government Printing Office, 1969) Vol. 115, Part 1, p. 329.

6. National Commission on Urban Problems, *Building the American City: Report to the Congress and to the President of the United States.* (Washington, D.C.: U.S. Government Printing Office, 1968), p. 325.

7. Denis F. Johnston, "Uptrend in Workers' Education," *Occupational Outlook Quarterly*, Vol. 7, No. 3 (September 1963), pp. 14-18.

8. National Research Council, Panel on Technology Assessment, *Technology: Processes of Assessment and Choice: Report of the National Academy of Sciences* (Washington, D.C.: U.S. Government Printing Office, 1969).

9. Jerome Wiesner, "Technology and Innovation," in Columbia University. Seminar on Technology and Social Change, *Technological Innovation and Society*, ed. by Dean Morse and Aaron W. Warner (New York: Columbia University Press, 1966), pp. 19-20.

10. Winston L. Prouty, "S.2769—Introduction of Human Investment Act of 1969," *Congressional Record* (Washington, D.C.: U.S. Government Printing Office, 1969), Vol. 115, Part 17, pp. 22293-22298.

11. Sylvia Porter, "Your Money's Worth: Schooling Worth 20 Years on Job," *The Evening Star*, Washington, D.C. (August 19, 1963), p. A-18.

12. John Holt, "Education for the Future," in Robert Theobald, ed., *Social Policies for America in the Seventies, Nine Divergent Views* (Garden City: Doubleday, 1968), pp. 181-182.

13. U.S. Congress. Senate. Committee on Government Operations, *Human Resources Development, Hearings Before the Subcommittee on Government Research; Deprivation and Personality—A New Challenge to Human Resources Development* (Washington, D.C.; U.S. Government Printing Office, 1968), Part 2, p. 246.

14. Donald N. Michael, "Social Impact of Technology," in Columbia University. Seminar on Technology and Social Change, *op. cit.*, p. 135-140.

15. U.S. Manpower Administration, *Seminar on Manpower Policy and Program: Psychological Dynamics of Inner City Problems*, by Ross Stagner (Washington, D.C.: U.S. Department of Labor, Manpower Administration, 1968), pp. 15-16.

16. Max Lerner, "Leisure Minus Work a Meaningless Equation," *The Evening Star*, (September 3, 1969), p. A-15.

17. Donald N. Michael, *op. cit.*

18. Helen M. Harris, "The Biggest Obstacle to Youth Employment," *The American Child*, Vol. 43, No. 3 (May 1961), pp. 1-4.

19. Conference on Unemployed, Out-of-School Youth in Urban Areas, *Social Dynamite; The Report* (Washington, D.C.: National Committee for Children and Youth, 1961), p. 17.

20. Donald N. Michael, *op. cit.*

21. *Ibid.*

22. Sylvia Porter, "Your Money's Worth: Plight of the Working Poor," *The Evening Star* (September 8, 1969), p. A-14.

23. U.S. Congress. Joint Economic Committee, *Employment and Manpower Problems in the Cities: Implications of the Report of the National Advisory Commission on Civil Disorders; Hearings* (Washington, D.C.: U.S. Government Printing Office, 1968).

24. Peter F. Drucker, "Managing the Educated," in Dan H. Fenn, ed., *Management's Mission in a New Society* (New York: McGraw-Hill, 1959), pp. 169ff.

25. Marcia K. Freedman, *The Process of Work Establishment*, (New York: Columbia University Press, 1969).

26. *Ibid.*

27. Princeton Manpower Symposium, *The Transition from School to Work; A Report* (Princeton: Princeton University, Industrial Relations Section, 1968): consensus of participants as recorded by author.

28. Bernard J. Bienvenu, "What Kind of Training for Tomorrow?" *Personnel,* Vol. 38, No. 6 (November/December 1961), pp. 8-17.

29. *Ibid.*

30. Samuel M. Burt and Herbert E. Striner, *Toward Greater Industry and Government Involvement in Manpower Development* (Kalamazoo: The W. E. Upjohn Institute for Employment Research, 1968).

Contributors

STERLING M. MCMURRIN is E.E. Ericksen Distinguished Professor and Dean of the Graduate School at the University of Utah. He has served on the faculty of the University of Southern California and has been Visiting Scholar at Columbia University and Union Theological Seminary and Ford Fellow in Philosophy at Princeton University. His wide government experience has included service as U.S. Commissioner of Education in 1961-62 and chairman of the Federal Commission on Instructional Technology. He is a trustee of the Carnegie Foundation and has been Vice President of the American Philosophical Association. McMurrin has also been a member of the CED Research Advisory Board, was project director of the recent CED subcommittees on Efficiency and Innovation in Education and Education for the Urban Disadvantaged, and is project director of the new subcommittee on the Management and Financing of Colleges. His writings include *A History of Philosophy* (with B.A.G. Fuller) and *Contemporary Philosophy* (with J.L. Jarrett).

GARTH L. MANGUM is McGraw Professor of Economics and Director of Economics and Director of the Human Resources Institute at the University of Utah. He is also Research Professor of Economics and Associate of the Center for Manpower Policy Studies at George Washington University, where he is directing an evaluation of federal manpower policies and programs financed by The Ford Foundation. In government, he has been a Senior Staff Analyst of the Presidential Railroad Commission; a special Mediator with the Federal Mediation and Conciliation Service; Research Director of the Senate Subcommittee on Employment and Manpower; Executive Director of the President's Committee on Manpower; and Executive Secretary of the National Commission on Technology, Automation, and Economic Progress. A native of Utah, Mangum received his doctorate at Harvard in 1960. He is a prolific author, his latest books being *The Emergence of Manpower Policy* and *Economic Opportunity in the Ghetto* (with Sar A. Levitan and Robert Taggart).

HOWARD A. MATTHEWS has been associated with the administration of the Manpower Development and Training Act since its inception in 1962. He served first as Chief of Program Operations in the Office of Education and since July 1966 has been Director of the program. Prior to joining the Office of Education, Matthews served in the public schools of Alaska in a number of administrative positions. As Assistant Commissioner for Institutional Services, he developed Alaska's first federally reimbursed vocational program. Later he was appointed Commissioner of Education for Alaska, which position he held when Alaska entered statehood. Matthews started his teaching career in 1947 as a high school teacher of history and economics. He received his master's degree from the University of Idaho in 1952 and his doctorate at George Washington University in 1964, having concentrated his program of studies in the field of administrative law.

RALPH W. TYLER has had a long and distinguished career in education, beginning with high school teaching in South Dakota in 1921 and leading through professorships at several universities to the University of Chicago, where for seventeen years he served in various posts, including Dean of the Division of Social Sciences. He was Director of the Center for Advanced Study in the Behavioral Sciences from 1953 to 1967 and is now Senior Consultant for Science Research Associates, Inc. He is chairman of a number of educational associations and commissions, among them the American College Testing Program, the National Commission for Cooperative Education, and the National Commission on Resources for Youth. He serves as a member of many other national, university, and school councils and committees.

SEYMOUR L. WOLFBEIN has been Professor of Economics and Dean of the School of Business at Temple University since 1967. For the twenty-two years prior to that he was with the U.S. Department of Labor, holding various important posts, including that of Chief of the Division of Manpower and Employment at the Bureau of Labor Statistics and Director of the Office of Manpower, Automation and Training. He is Chairman of the U.S. Regional Manpower Advisory Committee and a member of the Economic Advisory Board to the U.S. Secretary of Commerce, and has served on numerous boards and commissions in the field of manpower, training, and career guidance. Wolfbein has authored many articles and books, including *Education and Training for Full Employment* and *Occupational Information.*

Index